# HEARING GOD'S VOICE

*A practical guide to help people hear clearly from God*

BY

DR. BOBBY Y.K. SUNG

Copyright © 2015 **Dr. Bobby Y.K. Sung**

Published by Agape Behaviour publishing

All rights reserved

Unless otherwise indicated, all Scripture quotations are from The Holy Bible, New International Version

# Contents

Introduction to Hearing God's Voice ........................ 1

Appreciation ................................................. 3

About The Author ........................................... 4

Foreword .................................................... 5

# Chapters

1. We can hear His voice (Misconception vs. Truth) ......... 7
2. Relationship with God (We listen to God's voice) ........ 19
3. God's different ways to communicate .................. 33
4. God speaks to us through His Word ................... 45
5. God speaks to us through the inner prompting of the Holy Spirit .................................................. 61
6. God speaks to us through circumstances ............... 77
7. God speaks to us through visions ..................... 85
8. God speaks to us through dreams ..................... 93
9. God speaks to us through His creation ............... 101
10. God speaks to us through our five senses ............. 109
11. Jesus our example ................................... 121
12. How do we know it is God's voice? ................... 127
13. Practical ways of hearing His voice .................. 137
14. Hearing God's Voice (My personal encounter with God) . 147

# Introduction

# Hearing God's Voice

When my friend encouraged me to write a book, I asked myself what I should write about. What am I most passionate about? What is most important for our Christian Life? When I looked back at my Christian walk with God, and all the extraordinary things that has happened in my life, I realised that it is the voice of God that continues to spur my hunger for Him. It is hearing His sweet voice. Therefore listening to God's voice is very important in our spiritual life.

I write this book to encourage both my church members and you to connect with God. My heart is to help all who read this book to improve their ability to hear from God, and hear Him with confidence and clarity.

The testimonies in this book are from my true life and personal life experience of how I have heard God's voice. The examples mentioned are from my own genuine spiritual encounter with the Father that I would like to share with you.

I pray that you would be blessed by reading this book and that you will truly hear God's voice and come to know Him better through fellowship as your Heavenly Father.

We live in a 21st century society, where many extraordinary things has been happening. We have experienced a rapid growth in modern technology. Some may say that the world has become a much better place to live in. However, despite technological progression and societal modernisation, we still struggle with many issues, ranging from personal issues of finance, families and health to broader issues of politics, famine and war.

Many wish that a voice from heaven would speak to us and help us to solve all the problems, both Christians and non-Christians alike. We know that all solutions can be found in God, and desperately yearn to hear God's voice.

The questions many of us ask are these: Is it possible to hear God's voice? Does God still speak to us today? And how can we hear His voice?

# Appreciation

Thanks be to God, my heavenly Father, it is He who gave me the wisdom to write this book, all the resources I have are from Him.

I would like to thank all my church members including Yan, Mandy and Sarah who have helped me to translate this book. I would like to dedicate this book to my family, all my church members and to all those who love Jesus.

Thank you so much to Dr. Karen Chan for your excellent work and spending many hours to edit this book, God bless you.

Special thanks to my friend Dr. Mohammed T.S Johnson, teacher at www.theexceluniversity.org & senior pastor at Excel Centre Church, UK, he encouraged me to write the book, and helped me from start to finish on this project, God bless you.

Thanks also to my son Pastor Jonathan Sung for all your input with this book, God bless you.

I would like to lastly thank Bishop Francis for his spiritual covering. The Lord bless you Bishop.

# About The Author

Dr. Bobby Y.K Sung is the founder and Senior Pastor of Emmanuel Chinese church. He first encountered the Lord in Christmas 1986 after a friend shared the gospel with him. After receiving and accepting Jesus as his personal Lord and Saviour, he was filled with an earnest desire to share his newfound faith with everyone he met. His zeal and passion for the Lord inspired his family to know and follow Jesus Christ.

Shortly after his conversion, it became apparent that the Holy Spirit had baptised him in a completely unique and extraordinary manner. After being filled with the Spirit, Dr. Bobby Y.K Sung found himself naturally evangelising and ministering in a variety of supernatural spiritual gifts. Since the day of his salvation, the fire of God has burned incessantly in his heart. This is reflected in the rapid growth of his ministry as his passion for Jesus continues to ignite, inspire and touch the lives of many. In January 1999, he gave up his business in response to God's calling for him to serve in full time ministry. His greatest passions are reaching out to the lost, nurturing new believers and training passionate leaders of the Kingdom. Dr. Bobby Y.K Sung has three grown up children. His wife serves the Lord along side him as a great and powerful intercessor in the church.

This book will encourage and bless all people to hear the voice of God and develop their own relationship with Jesus. For more titles from this author see **www.ecclondon.com**

# Foreword

There are many books that have been written on the subject of 'Hearing God's Voice'. Most authors have concurred on how God speaks while on the other hand perspectives differ. Pastor Bobby Sung in his book **'Hearing God's Voice'** provides a unique and excellent thesis on the subject, giving clarity and provides a systematic guide that helps the reader on how to hear God effectively.

The opening prologue of Pastor Bobby's account deals with the misconceptions and aims to enlighten the reader that God still speaks today, not only to special individuals i.e. Prophets/Pastors and makes it clear that we all have the ability to hear God's voice.

The book depicts many examples on how God wants to communicate with us and how we can communicate with him in different ways and through various channels. 'Hearing God's Voice' affirms and supports its claims by providing scriptural references on how God communicated with the children of Israel in the Old Testament and the continuity of Him speaking in the New Testament.

Pastor Bobby shares his personal testimony on how reading the Word of God continually broke the power of alcohol and smoking addiction off his life. Soon after, God called him into full time ministry.

The book concludes with teaching on how to discern and know the voice of God and provides practical ways on how God's voice can be heard.

'**Hearing God's Voice**' *is simple and easy to read. I recommend this book to anyone who has a desire to hear God's voice. Pastor Bobby's unique account will certainly provide the tools you need to hear God clearly and frequently.* **Bishop John Francis, Ruach City Church, London UK**

*Rev. Dr. Bobby Sung is truly a man of God, I have witness his passion and love for people. Without a shadow of a doubt he hears from God. Just look at his life from being invited by distinguished leaders and people and ministering to thousands of people all over the world. I am fully convinced that this is a man that hears from God. This is indeed a practical guide to help people hear from the Almighty God.* **Dr. Mohammed T.S Johnson, Excel Centre Church, UK. www.theexceluniversity.org**

*This is the story of a man after God's heart. It speaks from a deep, intimate, heart-to-heart connection with God, built on encounter, faith, passion and a love for Jesus. This book will not only teach you how to hear from the Father, but will activate your spirit, unlock your heart and transform your life. It will reveal a new perspective on hearing from God, building on relationship and challenging current thinking for new and mature believers alike.* **Dr Karen Chan MBBS iBSc MRCP MA, member of Emmanuel Chinese Church, London UK.**

*This book inspires me to be sensitive to God's voice. After reading all the testimonies, I learned to walk closer to God through recognising His voice daily.* **Pastor Stephanie Fong Emmanuel Chinese Church.**

# Chapter 1

# We can hear His voice

*(Misconception vs. Truth)*

## – MISCONCEPTION 1 –

One common question asked by people – does God still speak to us after the completion of the Holy Scripture?

As a generation living in an age which benefits from the advantage of having the Bible, one very common misconception we have is that God has said all He wishes to say in His Word and therefore has nothing further to add.

## – TRUTH –

Although it is true that the written Word of God is complete, God continues to speak through his WORD.

When God completed the formation of Heaven and Earth, He rested on the seventh day. However, this does not imply that God stopped working. Although He was resting, He continued to work. Our Heavenly Father is always at work, and continues to work to this very day. In the same way, it is impossible to suggest that God has stopped speaking to people, as He has never stopped working!

## – MISCONCEPTION 2 –

The common myth is this: If God is the Creator of all things, holy, mighty and strong; how could we – mere mortals – possibly hear His voice?

## – TRUTH –

God created every human being in His own image and therefore desires all to hear His voice. He is always near to those who call on Him.

God is Almighty God, He is far away and yet He is near to us all. The Lord is near to those who call on him. **(Psalm 145:18)**

## – MISCONCEPTION 3 –

Many believe that the ability to hear God's voice is the exclusive privilege of appointed individuals, for example church leaders or those persistently praying in the cathedral.

They believe that only those who serve God, love God, seek God and pray fervently are worthy of the gift of receiving His word.

## – TRUTH –

I have witnessed many individuals who have flocked to those who claim to hear God's voice and have been called to serve as prophets. Huge crowds attend their special conferences in an attempt to seek God through these 'anointed' individuals. Whilst there is nothing wrong with us asking God to speak through His prophets, relying on prophets alone to hear from God can be problematic. Those individuals go to the prophets and pastors to ask about their career, their ministry and depend wholly on them for direction from God in their situation. They believe they can hear God only through the mouth of the prophet. However, these people do not seem to have considered one very tangible reality – that they can actually hear from God themselves.

The truth is that we all can hear God's voice – we do not need to chase conference after conference or seek the counsel of a famous prophet in order to hear Him.

## *Anyone can hear God's voice*

## – MISCONCEPTION 4 –

There are those who believe God is speaking to them every single time they read the Bible.

For the purpose of explanation and illustration I will use an example of an actual conversation that I had in the past with a new Christian believer.

I once asked a new Christian a question:

**Me:** *"What has God been saying to you recently?"*

**Tim:** *"God has been talking to me about Romans 1 today."*

**Me:** *"Is there anything in particular that He has spoken to you about?"*

**Tim:** *"God spoke to me about the whole of chapter 1."*

**Me:** *"The whole chapter?"*

**Tim:** *"Yes!"* (He said with excitement and certainty)

**Me:** *"Well, that's really amazing. God must have spoken to you about many things!"*

## – TRUTH –

The new believer believed that the chapter he had read from the Bible was literally what God was saying to him. I remain convinced that if he had read four chapters of Romans that day, he would have claimed that God had spoken to him on every word written in all four chapters that he had read.

It is possible that God can speak to us in a chapter, however this is not always the case as the Bible is also for us to learn from, it is not necessary that the whole chapter or book speaks directly to us.

Reading the Bible alone does not equate to listening to God's voice. Reading and listening are different.

God speaks to us by revelation through a Rhema Word (A Word from the Holy Spirit). Reading alone without hearing God's voice is merely reading.

*And how from infancy you have known the Holy Scriptures, which are able to make you wise for salvation through faith in Christ Jesus. All Scripture is God-breathed and is useful for teaching, rebuking, correcting and training in righteousness.* **(2 Timothy 3:15-16)**

## – MISCONCEPTION 5 –

Some say that God speaks only to His people, meaning born again Christians who believe in Jesus Christ.

## – TRUTH –

This is not quite true – God speaks to all of His creation, believers and non-believers.

**Examples from the Old Testament:**

**God spoke to Abimelech in a dream:**
*Now Abraham moved on from there into the region of the Negev and lived between Kadesh and Shur. For a while he stayed in Gerar, and there Abraham said of his wife Sarah, "She is my sister." Then Abimelech king of Gerar sent for Sarah and took her. But God came to Abimelech in a dream one night and said to him, "You are as good as dead because of the woman you have taken; she is a married woman.* **(Genesis 20: 1-3)**

**Examples from the New Testament:**

**God spoke to Pilate's wife:**
*While Pilate was sitting on the judge's seat, his wife sent him this message: "Don't have anything to do with that innocent man, for I have suffered a great deal today in a dream because of him.* **(Matthew 27: 19)**

Pilate's wife was a Roman. She was not Jewish and legitimately was not included in the covenant of God. She was a Gentile, yet still, God chose to speak to her. Furthermore, Pilate's wife received the message and recognised that the dream came from God.

**God spoke to Cornelius:**
*At Caesarea there was a man named Cornelius, a centurion in what was known as the Italian Regiment. He and all his family were devout and God-fearing; he gave generously to those in need and prayed to God regularly. One day at about three in the afternoon he had a vision. He distinctly saw an angel of God, who came to him and said, "Cornelius!" Cornelius stared at him in fear. "What is it, Lord?" he asked. The angel answered, "Your prayers and gifts to the poor have come up as a memorial offering before God. Now send men to Joppa to bring back a man named Simon who is called Peter.* **(Acts 10: 1-5)**

Cornelius saw visions and angels before he became a believer. God heard his prayer and spoke to him before he became a born again Christian. Like Pilate's wife, he was a Gentile. Again, Cornelius was not Jewish and would not have been covered by the covenant of God. However, far from overlooking him, God continued to love him and oversee all that he did. When God answered Cornelius' prayer, He enabled Cornelius to have a direct encounter with Him and hear His voice directly.

The previous examples clearly demonstrate that God speaks to different people at all times, in all places. The good news for our generation is this:

## God is still speaking to us all today

# Chapter 2
# Relationship with God

*(We listen to God's voice)*

## WE LISTEN TO HIS VOICE

*The watchman opens the gate for him, and the sheep listen to his voice. He calls his own sheep by name and leads them out.* **(John 10:3)**

*My sheep listen to my voice, I know them, and they follow me.* **(John 10: 27)**

We can hear God's voice all the time especially for direction, instruction and wisdom. Jesus clearly stated **"My sheep listen to my voice."** He did not say **"My sheep will probably hear my voice."** No! He said **"My sheep *listen* to my voice."** Therefore, all followers of Jesus can definitely hear His voice.

When an individual accepts Jesus Christ as his personal Lord and Saviour, he or she becomes His sheep. That person now belongs to Jesus and is God's child. Now he or she has reclaimed his identity as God's child, he or she can certainly hear God's voice.

*For God so loved the world that he gave his one and only Son that whoever believes in him shall not perish but have eternal life.* **(John 3: 16)**

## WE ARE CREATED FOR FELLOWSHIP WITH GOD

God loves each of us so much. He desires to have constant communication with us.

God created Adam and Eve for a purpose – to have fellowship with them. He did not create us to become mechanical robots.

When He created Adam, Then God said, *"Let us make man in our image, in our likeness, and let them rule over the fish of the sea, and the birds of the air, over the livestock, over all the earth, and over all the creatures that move along the ground." So, God created man in his own image, in the image of God he created him, male and female he created them. God blessed them and said to them, "Be fruitful and increase in number; fill the earth and subdue it. Rule over the fish of the sea and the birds of the air and over every living creature that moves on the ground."* **(Genesis 1: 26-28)**

God created us in His own image. He desires us to commune and have fellowship with Him. However, fellowship is not a single, one-sided monologue. Rather, it is a two-way, relational form of relationship and communication.

## GOD LOVES TO TALK

God is our Creator. However, He is also our Heavenly Father and loves to speak with us. Let us turn our attention to Genesis chapter 3. Here, Adam has eaten the forbidden fruit. He has sinned against God. Nevertheless, God, by his mercy and grace, was still looking for Adam to have fellowship with Him.

*Then the man and his wife heard the sound of the LORD God as he was walking in the garden in the cool of the day, and they hid from the LORD God among the trees of the garden. But the LORD God called to the man, "where are you?" He answer, "I heard you in the garden, and I was afraid because I was naked; so I hid." And he said, "Who told you that you were naked? Have you eaten from the tree that I commanded you not to eat from?"*

*The man said, "The woman you put here with me, she gave me some fruit from the tree, and I ate it." Then the LORD God said to the woman, what is this you have done?" The woman said, "The serpent deceived me, and I ate."* **(Genesis 3:8-13)**

After Adam and Eve ate the fruit from the tree, they fell short of the glory of God. Guilt and shame entered their lives, and they became very fearful. Although they heard the voice of God as He was walking in the garden, they tried to avoid God and hide themselves away from Him. But God is love, He created Adam and Eve in His own image. He created them for fellowship.

God loved Adam and Eve although they had sinned against Him. God's love never changes. This is evident from the scripture mentioned previously, which clearly highlights the effort God took to seek Adam and Eve. He clearly wished to commune and interact with them. This, in itself shows how long, wide, high and deep is God's love, that He still desires to have fellowship with those who have sinned against Him.

The book of Revelation reveals a further example of God's wish to communicate with us. Here, God declares:

*Here I am! I stand at the door and knock. If anyone hears my voice and opens the door, I will come in and eat with him, and he with me.* **(Revelation 3:20)**

Once again this scripture exemplifies God's desire to fellowship and communicate directly with us.

## GOD LOVES TO COMMUNICATE WITH US

The Bible contains many examples of people who heard God's voice. From the book of Genesis to the book of Revelation, there is mention of numerous individuals who heard God's voice and communicated with Him directly. All these people share one thing in common – they were human beings, just like us.

In the Old Testament *Abraham heard God's call.*

*God called Abraham out of Ur of Chaldeans to go to Canaan* **(Genesis 11: 31)**

**Moses heard God's voice in the burning bush.**
*When the LORD saw that he had gone over to look, God called to him from within the bush, "Moses! Moses!" And Moses said, "Here I am."* **(Exodus 3: 4)**

Elijah heard God's still small voice when he was downcast and wanted to end his life. He went into a cave and spent the night there. Then he heard the Lord speak to him in a small voice.

*After the earthquake came a fire, but the LORD was not in the fire. And after the fire came a gentle whisper. When Elijah heard it, he pulled his cloak over his face and went out and stood at the mouth of the cave. Then a voice said to him, "What are you doing here, Elijah?"* **(1 Kings 19: 12-13)**

In the New Testament Peter heard God's voice. God's instructions to Peter were: *"Get up, Peter. Kill and eat."* **(Acts 10: 13)**

This was not the only time that Peter heard the voice of God. In Acts 10:16, the same voice spoke to him a second time stating *"Do not call anything impure that God has made clean."*

**Paul also heard the voice of Jesus on his way to Damascus.**

*As he neared Damascus on his journey, suddenly a light from heaven flashed around him. He fell to the ground and heard a voice say to him, "Saul, Saul, why do you persecute me?"* **(Acts 9: 3-4)**

## JESUS CAME TO SPEAK TO US

Jesus came into this world, the WORD became flesh, and God became man.

He came to this world and became one of us.

*In the beginning was the Word, and the Word was with God, and the Word was God. He was with God in the beginning.* **(John 1:1)**

*Who, being in very nature God, did not consider equality with God something to be grasped, but made himself nothing, taking the very nature of a servant, being made in human likeness. And being found in appearance as a man, he humbled himself and became obedient to death even death on a cross!* **(Philippians 2:6-8)**

*Since the children have flesh and blood, he too shared in their humanity.* **(Hebrew 2:14)**

*He came to that which was his own, but his own did not receive him.* **(John 1:11)**

He came to speak to us, communicate to us, tell us the father's will, show us the father's work, and speak to us what he hears from the father.

*The Word became flesh and made his dwelling among us.* **(John 1:14)**

Jesus came to the world as the exact representation of the Father.

*The Son is the radiance of God's glory and the exact representation of his being, sustaining all things by his powerful word. After he had provided purification for sins, he sat down at the right hand of the Majesty in heaven.* **(Hebrews 1:3)**

*Anyone who has seen me has seen the Father.* **(John 14:9)**

*In the past God spoke to our forefathers through the prophets at many times and in various ways, but in these last days he has spoken to us by his Son, whom he appointed heir of all things, and through whom he made the universe.* **(Hebrews 1:1-2)**

Jesus is the Word. He came to speak to us, every word that comes from His mouth are life.

*THE Spirit gives life; the flesh counts for nothing. The words I have spoken to you are Spirit and they are life.* **(John 6:63)**

Jesus came to speak to the poor, to the rich, to the captives, to the sick, to the hopeless, to all kinds of people. Indeed, He came to interact with every single person in this world.

Since the fall of Adam, we constantly struggle to live a life that is pleasing to God, we all fall short of the glory of God and very often, we have no idea what God's will is for us.

In the Old Testament times, God used prophets and priests to speak to His people, and to teach them what God's law was. After many years, God finally sent His Son Jesus to the world to directly speak to us in person.

Many people are not sure how they should treat others. Society tell us "an eye for an eye and tooth for a tooth, love your neighbour and hate your enemy." But Jesus said *"do not resist an evil person, if someone strikes you on the right cheek, turn to him the other also. Love your enemies and pray for those who persecute you.* **(Matthew 5:38, 43, 44)**

***Jesus came to this world to speak to us and taught us how to live to please God. Even today, He continues to speak to us through His Holy Spirit.***

## THE FATHER AND SON RELATIONSHIP

Jesus connected us to the Father so that we could have fellowship with Him. He intended us to be able to speak with Him and hear His voice.

*Jesus answered, I am the way and the truth and the life. No one comes to the father except through me. If you really knew me, you would know my father as well, from now on; you do know him and have seen him.* (**John 14:6-7**)

*No one can come to me unless the Father who sent me draws him, and I will raise him up in the last day.* (**John 6:44**)

*All things have been committed to me by my Father. No one knows the Son except the Father, and no one knows the Father except the Son and those to whom the Son chooses to reveal him.* (**Matthew 11:27**)

When the disciples asked Jesus to teach them how to pray, Jesus said: "This, then, is how you should pray: *Our Father in heaven, hallowed be your name, your kingdom come, your will be done, on earth as it is in heaven. Give us today our daily bread. And forgive us our debts, as we also have forgiven our debtors. And lead us not into temptation, but deliver us from the evil one. For if you forgive other people when they sin against you, your heavenly Father will also forgive you. But if you do not forgive others their sins, your Father will not forgive your sins. "When you fast, do not look somber as the hypocrites do, for they disfigure their faces to show others they are fasting. Truly I tell you, they have received their reward in full. But when you fast, put oil on your head and wash your face, so that it will not be obvious to others that you are fasting, but only to your Father, who is unseen; and your Father, who sees what is done in secret, will reward you."* **(Matthew 6:9-18)**

Jesus connected us to our Heavenly Father. It is evident that Paul knew God as the Heavenly Father as in his epistles where he often referred to God as the Father.

*For this reason I kneel before the father* **(Ephesians 3:14)**

Our God is our Father in heaven; we have a very close, familial relationship with Him. Just as we communicate with our earthly fathers, we can also speak directly with our Heavenly Father. My belief is that knowing God as the Father stems entirely from a background of relationship, communication and fellowship.

Some may ask why did Jesus died on the cross to pay for our sins? The simple answer is that He died to reconcile us with our Heavenly Father and enable us to fellowship with Him!

It is important that when we communicate with Him, we understand that God is our Heavenly Father and not just our Creator.

It is true that the scriptures tell us that God is the Creator, the Almighty God, who is by His nature, Holy. However, if we focus only on God's mighty power and know Him solely as our Creator, we may begin to think that God's power distances us from Him. How can we, mere mortals, hear His voice? If we focus solely on God's holiness, surely we will never be worthy to come into His presence. Surely the Holy God does not wish to speak to the sinful? If we are to think in this way, our conversations with God would be filled with confessions of our sin.

However, knowing and understanding that God is our Heavenly Father provides a completely different perspective of God. A deeper knowledge of Him enables us to create an image of Father God in our mind.

We are therefore able to understand that God is love and He is filled with goodness and kindness. Having this perspective of God enables us to communicate freely with Him, not based on our status or ability, effort or merit but solely on account of what Jesus did for us on the cross. His sacrifice restored our relationship with the Father, so that we can now approach Him without fear, guilt or shame. His death allowed us to have true intimacy with Father God.

*Our God is a living God who loves to talk to us and desires us to clearly hear His voice!*

# *A close relationship with our Father God is not a religion*

# Chapter 3

# God's different ways to communicate

There are many different ways God can use to communicate to us. He is **omnipotent, omnipresent** and He is **omniscient**. This means that He is all powerful, He is everywhere, He is all knowing, and He is absolutely sovereign.

## GOD IS THE CREATOR OF ALL THINGS, HE IS SOVEREIGN.

We were created in God's image. Therefore God can choose from a number of ways to communicate with us. He can do all things. He knows what is good for us. He knows how to interact with us in such a way that we might be able to understand Him and hear His voice.

*There are so many different channels that God uses to speak to us and these are examples of a few:*

### 1. PRAYER

*In the church of Antioch there were prophets and teachers: Barnabas, Simeon called Niger, Lucius of Cyrene, Manaen (who had been brought up with Herod the tetrarch) and Saul. While they were worshiping the Lord and fasting, the Holy Spirit said, set apart for me Barnabas and Saul for the work to which I have called them.* **(Acts 13:2-3)**

*One of these days Jesus went out to a mountainside to pray, and spent the night praying to God, when the morning came, he called his disciples to him and chose twelve of them, whom he designated apostles.* **(Luke 6:12-13)**

## 2. COUNSEL

*Plans fail for lack of counsel, but with many advisers they succeed.* **(Proverbs 15:22)**

## 3. CIRCUMSTANCES

**(Genesis 37-50** *the life of Joseph and* **Genesis 45:4-8)** *Then Joseph said to his brothers, "Come close to me." When they had done so, he said, "I am your brother Joseph, the one you sold into Egypt! And now, do not be distressed and do not be angry with yourselves for selling me here, because it was to save lives that God sent me ahead of you. For two years now there has been famine in the land, and for the next five years there will be no plowing and reaping. But God sent me ahead of you to preserve for you a remnant on earth and to save your lives by a great deliverance. So then, it was not you who sent me here, but God. He made me father to Pharaoh, lord of his entire household and ruler of all Egypt.*

## 4. OPEN AND CLOSED DOORS

*But I will stay on at Ephesus until Pentecost, because a great door for effective work has opened to me, and there are many who oppose me.* **(1 Corinthians 16:8-9)**

*Paul and his companions travelled throughout the region of Phrygia and Galatia, having been kept by the Holy Spirit from preaching the word in the province of Asia. When they came to the border of Mysia, they tried to enter Bithynia, but the Spirit of Jesus would not allow them to. So they passed by Mysia and went down to Troas. During the night Paul had a vision of a man of Macedonia standing and begging him, "Come over to Macedonia and help us." After Paul had seen the vision, we got ready at once to leave for Macedonia, concluding that God had called us to preach the gospel to them.* **(Acts 16:6-10)**

## 5. AUDIBLE VOICE

*When the Lord saw that he had gone over to look, God called to him from within the bush, "Moses! Moses!" And Moses said, "Here I am."* **(Exodus 3:4)**

*He fell to the ground and heard a voice say to him, "Saul, Saul, why do you persecute me?"* **(Acts 9:4)**

## 6. ANGELS

*Then he lay down under the bush and fell asleep. All at once an angel touched him and said, "Get up and eat." He looked around, and there by his head was some bread baked over hot coals, and a jar of water. He ate and drank and then lay down again. The angel of the Lord came back a second time and touched him and said, "Get up and eat, for the journey is too much for you."* **(1 Kings 19:5-7)**

## 7. MIRACLES

*At the time of sacrifice, the prophet Elijah stepped forward and prayed: "Lord, the God of Abraham, Isaac and Israel, let it be known today that you are God in Israel and that I am your servant and have done all these things at your command. Answer me, Lord, answer me, so these people will know that you, Lord, are God, and that you are turning their hearts back again. Then the fire of the Lord fell and burned up the sacrifice, the wood, the stones and the soil, and also licked up the water in the trench. When all the people saw this, they fell prostrate and cried, "The Lord—he is God! The Lord—he is God!"* **(1 Kings 18:36-39)**

## 8. VISIONS

*After this, the word of the LORD came to Abram in a vision: "Do not be afraid, Abram I am your shield, your very great reward."* **(Genesis 15:1)**

## 9. DONKEYS

*But he was rebuked for his wrong doing by a donkey—an animal without speech—who spoke with a human voice and restrained the prophet's madness.* **(2 Peter 2: 16)**

## 10. DREAMS

*But God came to Abimelek in a dream one night and said to him, "You are as good as dead because of the woman you have taken; she is a married woman."* **(Genesis 20: 3)**

## 11. TRANCES

*About noon the following day as they were on their journey and approaching the city, Peter went up on the roof to pray. He became hungry and wanted something to eat, and while the meal was being prepared, he fell into a trance. He saw heaven* opened and something like a large sheet being let down to earth by its four corners. **(Acts 10: 9)**

## 12. GIFTS OF THE HOLY SPIRIT

But the one who prophesies speaks to people for their strengthening, encouraging and comfort. **(1 Corinthians 14:3)**

## 13. THE INNER VOICE OF THE HOLY SPIRIT

But when he, the Spirit of truth, comes, he will guide you into all the truth. He will not speak on his own; he will speak only what he hears, and he will tell you what is yet to come. **(John 16:13)**

So my God put it into my heart to assemble the nobles, **(Nehemiah 7:5)**

## 14. THE BIBLE

And how from infancy you have known the Holy Scriptures, which are able to make you wise for salvation through faith in Christ Jesus. All Scripture is God-breathed and is useful for teaching, rebuking, correcting and training in righteousness. **(2 Timothy 3:15-16)**

*Your word is a lamp for my feet, a light on my path.* (**Psalm 119:105**)

## 15. CREATION

*The heavens declare the glory of God; the skies proclaim the work of his hands. Day after day they pour forth speech; night after night they reveal knowledge. They have no speech, they use no words; no sound is heard from them. Yet their voice goes out into all the earth, their words to the ends of the world. In the heavens God has pitched a tent for the sun. It is like a bridegroom coming out of his chamber, like a champion rejoicing to run his course. It rises at one end of the heavens and makes its circuit to the other; nothing is deprived of its warmth.* (**Psalm 19:1-6**)

*For since the creation of the world God's invisible qualities—his eternal power and divine nature—have been clearly seen, being understood from what has been made, so that people are without excuse.* (**Romans 1:20**)

## 16. OTHERS

The Bible records many instances that God used individuals to speak His Word to another. Saul (Paul) and Ananias. (**Acts 9:10-18**)

*God can speak to us through any means, there is no restriction for Him, He can do as He pleases, and nothing can hinder His will. He can choose to speak to us at any time. His thoughts are higher than our thoughts.*

*As the heavens are higher than the earth, so are my ways higher than your ways and my thoughts than your thoughts.* **(Isaiah 55:9)**

When I first became a Christian, I was so hungry and thirsty for God. I wanted to be obedient to Him and do everything that He asked. As a new Christian, I wanted to know what God wanted me to do in my career and my future. I believe many of us also want to know God's will for our life, especially when we are new Christians.

I still remember clearly one Sunday, a week after I had received salvation, a man approached me after a morning service.

Though nothing particularly spectacular had happened during the service, a man came up to me afterwards and said "God said you should continue to do what you are doing right now". He even showed me a bible scripture that related to my situation. I believe that through that man, God spoke to me.

*The following chapters detail further some of the most common ways that God speaks to us*

# Chapter 4

# God speaks to us through His Word

God speaks to us through His Word. He has led me to the first step of hearing His voice – the reading of His Word, the Holy Bible.

*The grass withers and the flowers fall, but the word of our God stands forever.* **(Isaiah 40:8)**

*Your word, O LORD, is eternal, it stands firm in the heavens.* **(Psalm 119:89)**

*All scripture is God breathed and is useful for teaching, rebuking, correcting and training in righteousness.* **(2 Timothy 3:16)**

*I tell you the truth, until heaven and earth disappear, not the smallest letter, not the least stroke of a pen, will by any means disappear from the law until everything is accomplished.* **(Matthew 5:18)**

**There are two Greek words for the WORD:** *LOGOS and RHEMA –*

The Word of God is powerful – The Bible is the written Word of God, we call it Logos, which has already been completed.

God will not create another Bible as it has already been completed. Logos will never be changed.

Rhema is the spoken Word of God, a Word from the Holy Spirit, we call it the **'Now Word'**. It is what God is saying to us now!

## HOW DOES HE SPEAK TO US?

When we read, study and meditate God's written Word, the Holy Spirit will come and stir up His written Word in our hearts. This is when His written Word comes to life, and Logos becomes Rhema. Let me take raw rice as an example. Raw (uncooked) rice is exactly what you can see-small grains of hard rice which cannot be consumed unless cooked first. The same can be true of the Word. The Word of God in its raw form can be of limited use to us if we are unable to comprehend it. Only after God speaks to us through His Word, does it come to life within us and become a Word that is relevant to us today.

God speaks to us through His written WORD.

*Is not my word like fire, declares the LORD, and like a hammer that breaks a rock in pieces?* **(Jeremiah 23:29)**

*They asked each other, "were not our hearts burning within us while he talked with us on the road and opened the scriptures to us?"* **(Luke 24:32)**

*For the word of God is living and active. Sharper than any double- edged sword, it penetrates even to dividing soul and spirit, joints and marrow, it judges the thoughts and attitudes of the heart.* **(Hebrews 4:12)**

When Jesus was explaining the scriptures to the two disciples on the road, their hearts burned as though a fire was alight inside of them. God's Word was active, it penetrated into their spirit, stirring something deep inside of them. Flames burned in their hearts. The spectacular power of God's word gave them a sensation of heat and burning. Jeremiah also described a similar experience in the Old Testament.

*His word is in my heart like fire, a fire shut up in my bones. I am weary of holding it in; indeed, I cannot.* **(Jeremiah 20:9).**

When I first became a Christian, I was so excited about my newfound faith. Everything was new and fresh to me, but what I found particularly fascinating was the revelation that I now co-inhabited two worlds simultaneously– that of the physical and spiritual realm. Without receiving formal instruction from others, I found myself supernaturally able to hear God's voice.

After accepting Jesus, I was so hungry for God and desperately wanted to read His Word to find out more about Him. However, I did not have a Bible. By the grace of God, I later received a 'Good News Version' Bible from my friend as a Christmas present. I loved the Bible so much that I read it day and night. I slept very little each day and was convinced that this was the best book in the world. In my mind, no other book could compare. Although I did not understand what the Bible was saying, I really enjoyed reading the Word of God.

Let me tell you something interesting. I used to drink and smoke. I would read the Bible in one hand and hold my cigarettes and alcohol in the other. Despite this, I thoroughly enjoyed reading the Word of God. It is hard for me to imagine now how I had so much energy and strength to read the Bible. Looking back, it was the Holy Spirit who empowered me and enabled me to read the whole Bible (from the first page of Genesis to the last page of Revelation) in just four weeks.

One particularly poignant memory of my experience as a new believer is as follows. I was reading **1 Corinthians 3:16** which states: *"Don't you know that you yourselves are God's temple and that God's Spirit lives in you?"*

This was later followed by **1 Corinthians 6:19:** *"Do you not know that your body is a temple of the Holy Spirit, who is in you, whom you have received from God? You are not your own"*.

When I read these two verses, my heart began to pound as if there was something very hot inside of me. I was frightened, but not in a sceptical manner. I had been filled with a Godly sense of mind. I was in awe! As I repeatedly read the same verses, I wanted to be sure that I was not misunderstanding the Word. At that moment something indescribable happened in my heart. I felt an intense heat, like fire and at first I thought I had a temperature. I was restless and could not sit still because I was so hot. At that time I did not realise that it was the Holy Spirit stirring inside of me. The Words *"your body is the temple of the Holy Spirit"* really struck me.

God's written Word (Logos) had come alive (Rhema). My response was to immediately throw away my cigarettes. Even though there were plenty remaining in the pack, I threw them all into the dustbin together with my ashtray. I was a heavy smoker and had begun to smoke at the age of 12. Although I had tried to quit smoking on many occasions, I had never been able to successfully give up. However, that night as I read the Word of God telling me that my body is the temple of God, I felt God speak to me directly through His written Word. The Word hit me so abruptly and struck me so deeply that I knew from deep within my heart that God had spoken to me directly.

My experience with our Heavenly Father that day had a deep impact in my heart. Since that encounter, there is nothing I enjoy more than spending time reading His Word, enjoying His presence and listening to His voice.

God also used His written Word to speak to me when He called me into full time ministry. I was reading **John 21:17:** *"Feed my sheep"*. The Word hit me and again stirred something inside my heart. My heart leapt and I knew that it was God speaking to me. I could recognise His voice.

On another occasion, I had been reading the same chapter repeatedly for several days. I felt that God was drawing my attention to that chapter. I loved reading it again and again because I knew God was speaking to me. He wanted me to memorise the whole chapter, and I did so.

Whenever I heard God's voice, I would respond to it with faith. Consequently, God was able to lead me to another level of learning to hear His voice. God has never stopped training me in this. The key to hearing God's voice is faith and it is by faith that we respond to His voice.

Consequently, faith comes from hearing the message, and the message is heard through the word about Christ. **(Romans 10:17)**

It is imperative that we respond to His Word. If we do what He asks us to do, He will continue to speak to us and lead us to another level in hearing His voice.

When God was calling Abraham out of his hometown and country, He did not give Abraham much detail of where to go.

The Lord had said to Abram, leave your country, your people and your father's household and go to the land I will show you. **(Genesis 12:1)**

God did not tell Abraham where to go. God only told him to go to the land that He will show him!

Abraham was obedient and responded to God's call. Consequently God spoke to him again and again, in chapter 15 God spoke to him again and giving him visions and revealing more detail of his calling to him. **(Genesis 15:1-4)**

Paul heard the voice of Jesus on his way to Damascus. *Jesus told him to get up and go into the city, where he would receive further instruction* **(Acts 9:5)**

Paul was a high ranking Roman soldier who had been persecuting Christians. When he was about to arrest Christians on his way to Damascus, Jesus appeared to him and he was converted. He heard the voice of Jesus telling him to get up and go into the city. Paul obeyed Jesus' voice. As he obeyed in faith, God revealed more to him. He saw a vision whilst praying **(Acts 9:12)**. This vision revealed that a man named Ananias would come and place his hands on him to restore his sight.

Every step of obedience leads to a deeper and more intimate knowledge of God. Obedience to His Word is important.

God has used His Word to speak to me on many occasions. One thing is for certain: when He speaks to us, He will ensure that we can hear His voice.

Let me give you an example, in the book of Samuel **(1 Samuel 3:1-19)**, which records a young boy, his name is Samuel. God spoke to him many times, the first three times, he did not know it was God speaking to him, this was because he had never heard God's voice before and therefore was unable to recognise His voice. However God really wanted to speak to Samuel, and so God made sure that Samuel heard His voice clearly.

He spoke to him the fourth time, God called his name 'Samuel', 'Samuel', and Samuel responded to God by saying, "Speak Lord, for your servant is listening." This time he could hear His voice clearly.

God patiently spoke to Samuel again and again until he was able to distinguish the voice he was hearing as God.

When God speaks to us, He will ensure that we can hear His voice, don't worry if you miss His voice the first time, God will make sure you will be able to hear it clearly the next time.

## GOD USES BOTH HIS WRITTEN WORD (LOGOS) AND HIS VOICE TO SPEAK TO US (RHEMA).

It is very important to read His word every day. *Like new born babies, crave for pure spiritual milk, so that by it you may grow up in your salvation.* **(1 Peter 2:2)**

When you read His Word, God may draw your attention to a particular verse or passage and that verse or passage may have particular meaning or application to your life.

For example, say one day you have bitterness in your heart. On reading the Bible, God suddenly draws your attention to **(Ephesians 4:31)** *which states: "Get rid of all bitterness, rage and anger, brawling and slander, along with every form of malice."* God may be using this bible verse to speak to you about the bitterness you are currently harbouring inside of you.

Therefore reading His Word is important, God uses His Word to speak to us. Read it and be familiar with His Word, memorise His Word, *let the*

*Word of Christ dwell in you richly as you teach and admonish one another with all wisdom, and as you sing psalms, hymns and spiritual songs with gratitude in your hearts to God.* **(Colossians 3:16)**

It is important to store up God's Word in our hearts so that God can use it to communicate with us. For instance, if a computer does not have any software installed, it cannot do the things we want it to do!

The same is true for Christians. If we do not have the Word of God rooted in us like a software. God may wish to use His word to communicate with us, but on searching our hard drive, find nothing. He is simply unable to use His own Word to communicate us.

I encourage you to read His word. Study it, memorise it, meditate on it and be a doer of His word. The more we store in our hearts, the richer we will be and the more channels we will have for God to speak to us. God can speak to us at any time, when we meditate His Word, during our study of His Word, or when we are memorising His Word.

The scripture is a common method that God uses to speak to us. Many people desire to hear His voice but are not willing to spend time with Him to read His Word. They want a quick fix like cooking instant noodles. They just want God to tell them simple points and state a, b and c. However, they have never paused in their busy lives to consider investing time to read the Word of God. If we have never picked up the Bible to read, how can God speak to us? It is not that He does not want to speak to us – He definitely wants to speak to us but we need to read His Word. He uses His written Word to communicate with us. I believe this is the way He speaks to us most of the time.

## HAVE A GREAT ATTITUDE LIKE KING DAVID

**Longing for God's Word:** *He is longing for His Word more than gold and more than pure gold.* **(Psalm 119:127)**

*My soul is consumed with longing for your laws at all times.* **(Psalm 119:20)**

*How I long for your precepts* **(Psalm119:40)**

*I open my mouth and pant, longing for your commands* **(Psalm 119:131)**

*The law from your mouth is more precious to me than thousands of pieces of silver and gold.* **(Psalm 119:72)**

**Meditate on His Word:**

*Though rulers sit together and slander me, your servant will meditate on your decrees.* **(Psalm 119:23)**

*I meditate on your precepts and consider your ways* **(Psalm 119:15)**

**Hidden His word:**

*I have hidden your word in my heart* **(Psalm 119:11)**

*Rejoice in His Word:*

*I rejoice in following your statutes as one rejoices in great riches.* **(Psalm 119:14)**

As you can see King David loved God's Word, his heart was always longing to hear God's voice, this was always an open invitation for God to speak to King David and for King David to hear the King of King's voice.

As I said earlier God speaks to us through His Word. It is a fundamental step to hear His voice and enter into the supernatural realm; He uses His written Word to speak to us, to train our mind to be sensitive to His advice. It is the most common way that God communicates to us.

When you are reading the Bible, you are doing a supernatural thing. Yes, indeed, you are doing a spiritual thing. You are reading God's word, and His Word is Spirit and life. His Word is from heaven. Position yourself in such a way as though you can see Jesus sitting before you. Ask Him to speak to you and to open the eyes of your heart, so that you may see the wonderful things in His Word. Ask Him to give you revelation so that you may know Him better and hear His voice.

# We need to come to His presence and read His Word if we want to hear His voice

# Chapter 5

# God speaks to us through the inner prompting of the Holy Spirit

*But the counsellor, the Holy Spirit, whom the Father will send in my name, will teach you all things and will remind you of everything I have said to you.* **(John 14:26)**

*You, however, are controlled not by the sinful nature but by the Spirit, if the Spirit of God lives in you. And if anyone does not have the Spirit of Christ, he does not belong to Christ, he does not belong to Christ. But if Christ in you, your body is dead because of sin, yet your spirit is alive because of righteousness. And if the Spirit of him who raised Jesus from the dead is living in you, he who raised Christ from the dead will also give life to your mortal bodies through his Spirit, who lives in you.* **(Roman 8:9-11)**

The moment we accept Christ, the Holy Spirit immediately comes and dwells in us. He is our helper, advocate, comforter and counsellor. He quickens our spirit and brings us to life. Before we became Christians, we have no interest in the spiritual realm. We are dead in our transgressions. However, after we are reborn in Christ and receive the Holy Spirit, He makes everything come to life. It is as though there is breakthrough in every channel of our life, with no obstructions or blockages. This is because the Holy Spirit now lives in us.

**Jesus said to his disciples:**
*And I will ask the Father, and he will give you another*

*counsellor to be with you forever, the Spirit of truth. The world cannot accept him, because it neither sees him nor knows him. But you know him, for he lives with you and will be in you.* **(John 14:16-17)**

The Holy Spirit dwells inside every believer. His main role is to help us and remind us of all Jesus has said, is saying and will say in the future. The Holy Spirit is Jesus' representative. He is responsible for informing us of Jesus' plans for us as well as helping us to minister.

*But the counsellor, the Holy Spirit, whom the Father will send in my name, will teach you all things and will remind you of everything I have said to you* **(John 14:26)**

*But when he, the Spirit of truth, comes, he will guide you into all truth, he will not speak on his own, he will speaks only what he hears, and he will tell you what is yet to come.* **(John 16:13)**

*All that belongs to the Father is mine, that is why I said the Spirit will take from what is mine and make it known to you* **(John 16:15)**

Praise God! We have the Holy Spirit living inside us and God can speak to us through the Holy Spirit.

*It had been revealed to him by the Holy Spirit that he would not die before he had seen the Lord's Christ. Moved by the Holy Spirit, he went into the temple courts. When the parents brought in the child Jesus to the temple to do for him what the custom of the law required.* **(Luke 2:26-27)**

Simeon was a righteous and devout Jew who was filled with the Holy Spirit, and it was the Holy Spirit who revealed that he would see the Messiah before his death. The Scripture reveals that Simeon had been waiting for the Messiah for a while. For exactly how long he had been waiting is unclear, but the Spirit gave Simeon special insight and knowledge so that he would recognise the "Messiah." One day, he was prompted by the Spirit to enter the temple courts. It was here that Simeon found Jesus and his parents at the temple. This was at exactly the right time and location. Some may think this was merely a coincidence, but I believe what was written in the Bible. Simeon's heart had been touched by the Holy Spirit and this is why he chose to enter the temple at that particular time and place.

*And now compelled by the Spirit, I am going to Jerusalem, not knowing what will happen to me there. I only know that in every city the Holy Spirit warns me that prison and hardship are facing me. However I consider my life worth nothing to me, if only I may finish the race and complete the task the Lord Jesus has given me, the task of testifying to the gospel of God's grace.* **(Acts 20:22-24)**

After spreading the gospel to the Gentiles and planting many churches, Paul felt the Spirit urge him to travel to Jerusalem. He was convinced that the Holy Spirit had not only spoken to him, but compelled him to move in this direction with God. After Paul's encounter with the Holy Spirit, he knew that many dangers lay ahead. Many warned Paul of the risks and danger and pleaded with him not to go. The prophet Agabus even journeyed from Judea to warn him of the troubles that lay ahead. However, Paul was certain of what he had heard and stated that he was willing to die in Jerusalem. **(Acts 21:10-14)** Paul's conviction from the Holy Spirit was so strong that he did not even care about his own life. He was certain that he had heard from the Spirit correctly, and therefore was willing to risk his own life in order to fulfil the command given to him by God.

One personal encounter I have had of being prompted by the Holy Spirit goes back to my early days as a Christian. As I prepared to leave church after the end of Sunday service, I felt the Holy Spirit speaking to my heart. I felt an unusual stirring and feeling of compulsion inside me. For an unknown reason, I felt a strong urge to walk alongside a certain young man. I quickly followed this particular individual and started a conversation with him. I asked him what he thought of the service and he told me that he too was a new Christian. He seemed very sad and downcast and actually said to me *"If you did not speak to me, I would have gone to the cemetery and sat there to mediate on the sermon."*

After sharing more, it transpired that he was struggling with his faith. He found it very difficult to do and obey God's Word. I invited him to my house. My wife greeted us on our arrival, and was surprised that I brought a random gentleman to our house! However, that night we had a good and in depth conversation. After our talk, the young man felt a sense of release.

As a two to three month old Christian, I did not fully understand who or what the Holy Spirit was, but I was willing to follow the prompting of the Holy Spirit.

I obeyed the Holy Spirit and did something out of character for myself. Looking back, this experience helped me to realise that the Holy Spirit really loves each of us so much. He loved the young man so much, He asked me to walk alongside him and help him.

On another occasion, I was walking in China Town when I spotted a Chinese man buying some medicine. Again, I felt the prompting of the Holy Spirit and had the same feeling that I had previously experienced with the young man outside church. I felt an urge to follow this man.

The Chinese man was neither special nor suspicious, but I felt a strong need to follow him. I followed him wherever he went, just as a detective follows a suspect. He boarded a bus, and I followed him. When he got off at St Thomas' hospital, I continued to follow him, even following him into a lift! However, when he entered the ward, I found myself in a slightly strange position as I had no one to visit.

At that moment, it seemed like I had followed this Chinese gentleman for absolutely no reason. I was standing on the ward like an idiot, when suddenly I heard a voice shout my name *"Pastor Bobby!"* As soon as I heard my name, I turned around and saw my church member in a patient bed. She was so happy and excited to see me. She asked me if I had come to visit her and wondered how I knew she had been admitted to hospital. To be completely honest, I had no idea why she was in hospital. It turned out she had been brought to hospital by ambulance because she had jumped from the second floor of a building and broken her leg.

It was by God's everlasting love and grace that the Holy Spirit led me to follow the Chinese man to hospital and unexpectedly pay her a visit. Again, the Holy Spirit prompted me deep within my heart. He compelled me to do some seemingly strange things that were completely out of character for me. To any normal person, it would seem ridiculous to randomly follow a complete stranger, but the Holy Spirit knows everything.

As Christians, we are able to discern and follow the leading of the Holy Spirit because he lives and dwells in us. The Holy Spirit can speak to us at any time and place, therefore we must learn to become more sensitive to His prompting and ways of communicating to us. In both these situations, whenever Holy Spirit spoke to me, I felt a stirring in my heart. Over time, I have learned to recognise these incidences and act upon these promptings immediately.

Some might question whether these feelings are from God or our own thoughts. Well, we often focus on our own feelings, but do not realise, we are also a spiritual being and the Holy Spirit dwells in us. Feelings can be from the Holy Spirit. If what you hear is from God then it is impossible for you not to experience Him. Your obedience will result in an increase in your faith. If what you hear is not from God, you have nothing to lose except your own *"face"* – this is a traditional Chinese saying which implies embarrassment. As Paul wrote *"we live by faith and not by sight."* We should always remember that we are God's beloved children. He loves us all so much and always wishes to speak with us. He will continue to train us to recognise His voice at any time or place.

On yet another occasion, I heard the voice of God telling me to say a public prayer. I was a young Christian and again I felt the Holy Spirit speaking deep in my heart and telling me to pray out loud. At that time, the Pastor was actively encouraging the congregation to pray out loud during worship. I was afraid because the church was packed with over 200 people attending and I was the only Chinese person there. My English wasn't very good, so I struggled with myself for a few minutes, but eventually decided to give in and keep my mouth shut.

You can imagine my surprise when another man in the congregation prayed exactly the things that were on my heart. I realised I had missed the opportunity that God had given me to pray. The next Sunday, I again felt Holy Spirit stirring in my heart and prompting me to pray out loud. Yet again, I reluctantly withdrew from the opportunity and closed my mouth.

However our God is a gracious God. He spoke to me again on the third Sunday and prompted me through the Holy Spirit. This time I responded to his voice and chose to obey and pray out loud by faith. After doing so, I felt immediately relieved, like a heavy burden had been lifted off me. I felt so happy and had so much joy in my heart when I released that prayer. From this, I learned that the Holy Spirit speaks to us, even though other people may not have heard. When He speaks, we know deep down in our hearts that we have heard from Him and sometimes cannot explain it. We just know!

I recall one Sunday morning many years ago, also in my early Christian life, I was driving to church with my family. During the drive, I felt the prompting of the Holy Spirit in my heart when I stopped at a red light halfway to church. I had an impression (spiritual feeling) that the Holy Spirit was telling me that something was wrong with the water tank on my rooftop. As soon as I heard His voice, I immediately shared these thoughts with my wife and my three children. I told them that we could not stay for fellowship and should return home once the service had finished.

Much to my dismay, my family laughed at me. They jokingly asked why God had spoken only to me but not to them. They even asked questions such as "How did God speak to you? What did his voice sound like? Did God speak Chinese, English, Hebrew or Greek to you?" I explained that God spoke deep in my heart, but my family simply didn't believe me. However, deep in my heart, I was certain God had spoken to me, and my previous experiences had taught me to recognise His voice and not to dismiss it as my own imagination. As head of the household, they reluctantly obeyed me and as soon as service ended, we returned immediately to our home.

On arrival to my home, the first thing I did was check the water tank and the condition was exactly what the Holy Spirit had told me earlier in the morning. It was horrible! The water tank was extremely dirty and the wood had rotten also allowing rain water to get into the tank. We could not believe that we had used this water to bathe everyday unquestioningly. Praise the Lord! God knows everything in our lives! That day, we all praised God for speaking to me.

One further example was two years ago when I was driving to church on Sunday. I did not know why, but I kept singing the same song. The lyrics included the words *"save me, protect me."* During the drive, I stopped at a traffic light and I heard the Spirit of God say to my heart *"Don't go."* Strangely enough, the traffic light was green and both the vehicles on my left and right drove away leaving me at the traffic light. Suddenly, a car from the crossroad crashed dramatically into the car on my right, consequently colliding with the car on my left. All three cars were spinning round and round, yet my car was still stationary at the traffic light. Hallelujah! I could have been in this accident, but God saved my life. By knowing His voice and obeying Him, the Holy Spirit saved my life.

In the book of Ezekiel: *Some of the elders of Israel came to me and sat down in front of me, then the word of the Lord came to me: "Son of man, these men have set up idols in their hearts and put wicked stumbling blocks before their faces, Should I let them enquire of me at all ?* **(Ezekiel 14:1-3)**

God was speaking to Ezekiel while he was sitting in front of the elders. The elders did not hear anything, only Ezekiel heard the voice of God. God did not speak with a voice audible to all, implying that it was an inner voice – it was the Spirit who spoke in Ezekiel's heart.

**Example of Elijah.**

*The LORD said," Go out and stand on the mountain in the presence of the LORD, for the LORD is about to pass by." Then a great and powerful wind tore the mountain apart and shattered the rocks before the LORD, but the LORD was not in the wind. After the wind there was earthquake, but the LORD was not in the earthquake. After the earthquake came a fire, but the LORD was not in the fire. And after the fire came a gentle whisper. When Elijah heard it, he pulled his cloak over his face and went out and stood at the mouth of the cave. Then a voice said to him," What are you doing here, Elijah?"* **(1 Kings 19:11-13)**

Elijah was discouraged, depressed and wanted to end his life, God spoke to him in a still small voice. God did not speak to him through earthquake, wind or fire. It could well be that God spoke in his heart.

**Another example is that of Nehemiah.**

*I set out during the night with a few men. I had not told anyone what my God had put in my heart to do for Jerusalem. There were no mounts with me except the one I was riding on.* **(Nehemiah 2:12)**

*So my God put it into my heart to assemble the nobles, the officials and the common people for registration by families.* **(Nehemiah 7:5)**

Nehemiah mentioned twice that God put it into his heart. When the Holy Spirit speaks into our hearts, no one else can hear what He is saying. Others are not able to hear because God is speaking directly to your heart.

You may ask how the Holy Spirit works in our heart? Well, God is Spirit, just as we are both physical beings and spiritual beings. As God is Spirit He communicates with us through His Holy Spirit, His ***Spirit*** to our ***spirit***. Sometimes, He may give us a burden to pray, or He may whisper in a still small voice within our hearts or He may give us an impression of something (spiritual feeling).

That is why it is very important to become sensitive to the Holy Spirit's prompting in your heart. You must cultivate a habit of responding whenever you feel the Holy Spirit is speaking to you. Do whatever He asks of you even though it might seem strange at first. Obey His instruction and walk by faith. The more you practice this, the more sensitive you will become. When you begin to obey His voice, I am certain that God will continue to help you grow to a higher level of hearing His voice.

# Chapter 6

# God speaks to us through circumstances

*But I will stay on at Ephesus until Pentecost, because a great door for effective work has opened to me, and there are many who oppose me.* **(1 Corinthians 16:8-9)**

*Paul and his companions travelled throughout the region of Phrygia and Galatia, having been kept by the Holy Spirit from preaching the word in the province of Asia. When they came to the border of Mysia, they tried to enter Bithynia, but the Spirit of Jesus would not allow them to. So they passed by Mysia and went down to Troas. During the night Paul had a vision of a man of Macedonia and begging him, "Come over to Macedonia and help us," After Paul had seen the vision, we got ready at once to leave for Macedonia, concluding that God had called us to preach the gospel to them.* **(Acts 16:6-10)**

God spoke to Paul by opening and closing doors. The Holy Spirit prevented him from preaching in the province of Asia, He used circumstances to speak to him.

*Then he prayed, O LORD, God of my master Abraham, give me success today, and show kindness to my master Abraham. See, I am standing beside this spring, and the daughters of the townspeople are coming out to draw water. May it be that when I say to a girl, please let down your jar that I may have a drink, and she says, 'Drink, and I will water your camels too,' let her be the one you have chosen for your servant Isaac. By this I will know that you have kindness to my master. Before he had finished praying, Rebekah came out with her jar on her shoulder.* **(Genesis 24:12-15)**

*Without saying a word, the man watched her closely to learn whether or not the LORD had made his journey successful.* **(Genesis 24:21)**

*Saying, "Praise the LORD, the God of my master Abraham, who has not abandoned his kindness and faithfulness to my master. As for me, the LORD has led me on the journey to the house of my master's relatives."* **(Genesis 24:27)**

Here, God used circumstances to guide Abraham's servant. He monitored the situation and watched what Rebekah was doing. Rebekah was drawing water for the camels. When we consider this in more depth, we begin to understand that at that time, drawing water for a stranger was a normal and customary thing to do, drawing water for ten camels was not. The camels must have needed many gallons of water, and this would have been very time consuming for Rebekah, thereby making it an unusual and extraordinary incident. I believe that it was not a coincidence that Rebekah spent so much time and effort drawing water for the ten camels. God was working behind the scenes, orchestrating everything that was happening. It aligned with what Abraham's servant had prayed for. God used the circumstance to speak to him and guide him, so that the servant would know that it was God's will for Isaac to take Rebekah as his wife. God spoke to Abraham's servant through situation and circumstance.

When God called me to serve in full-time ministry, I heard His voice through reading His word. *"Feed my sheep."* **(John 21:15-17)**

When God called me to serve him, I was a business owner. However, when I received the calling, I was extremely excited. I felt that it was a privilege and honour to serve the mighty God, the Creator of all things. I was willing to obey His voice immediately, but I also wanted to discern if what I was hearing was truly His calling in my life? Did God really want me to give up my business and serve in full time ministry? It was a big life changing decision.

I spoke to God and said: *"Lord, if it is you who has called me to serve in full time ministry, please send someone to buy my shop without me needing to advertise it on the market."* Much to my surprise, the day after praying to the Lord, someone came into my shop and asked if I would sell my business. When I enquired about how he knew of my intentions of selling the business, he stated that no one had told him anything. He simply wanted to start a business in the area, and he had been sitting in his car, observing my business over the last few days. It was God who directed all things, just as it says in the Bible *'the king's heart is in the hand of the Lord, He directs it like a watercourse wherever he pleases.'* **(Proverbs 21:1)**

I asked the Lord again: *"Lord, I know it is you who called me to serve. However, I need a house to live in, as we are currently living above our shop. Although we own another property, it is rented out under a contract which was only signed a few weeks ago."* I asked God: *"Lord, what should I do? If I sell my business, we will have nowhere to live."* After a few days, I received a telephone call from the tenant who was renting my house. He told me that he would need to move out in a few weeks time because the council offered him a different property. He had no choice but to break the contract and leave my property.

God was behind all these things. He orchestrated everything behind the scenes so things would work out perfectly. He used the circumstances to communicate with me, allowing me to realise that it was Him who was speaking.

Let us look at another example, in the Old Testament, in the book of Exodus, it was evident that God used circumstance to convince Pharaoh to set God's people free from slavery, but Pharaoh refused to listen.

Our God is the creator of all things, His eyes is everywhere, nothing is hidden in His sight.

*For He spoke, and it came to be, he commanded, and it stood firm.* **(Psalm 33:9)**

*As I quoted before even the king's heart is in the hand of the Lord; He directs it like a watercourse wherever He pleases.* **(Proverb 21:1)**

## GOD DOES USE CIRCUMSTANCES TO SPEAK TO US

It is worth noting that *God does use circumstances to speak to us*. Therefore, we need to watch and pay attention to what God is doing in every situation. Whether we face financial difficulty, business failure, or experience sickness, God can use all of these situations to speak to us. However although God uses circumstances, we need to discern God's will carefully within the situation. Some circumstances may not always be God's will. Therefore it is important to remember not to rush! Pray about the situation and bring all matters before Him. As in the book of Proverbs states it clearly, *"Trust in the* Lord *with all your heart and lean not on your own understanding."* **(Proverbs 3:5)**

# Chapter 7

# God speaks to us through visions

*After this, the word of the LORD came to Abram in a vision: "Do not be afraid, Abram, I am your shield, your very great reward."* **(Genesis 15:1)**

*Then the word of the LORD came to him: "This man will not be your heir, but a son coming from your own body will be your heir." He took him outside and said, "Look up at the heavens and count the stars- if indeed you can count them," Then he said to him, "So shall your offspring be."* **(Genesis 15:4-5)**

*At Caesarea there was a man named Cornelius, a Centurion in what was known as the Italian Regiment. He and all his family were devout and God fearing, he gave generously to those in need and prayed to God regularly. One day at about three in the afternoon he had a vision. He distinctly saw an angel of God, who came to him and said, "Cornelius!" Cornelius stared at him in fear, "what is it Lord?" He asked.* **(Acts 10:3-4)**

*About noon the following day as they were on their journey and approaching the city, Peter went up on the roof to pray. He became hungry and wanted something to eat, and while the meal was being prepared, he fell into a trance. He saw heaven opened and something like a large sheet being let down to earth by its four corners.* **(Acts 10:9-11)**

*While Peter was wondering about the meaning of the vision, the men sent by Cornelius found out where Simon's house was and stopped at the gate.* **(Acts 10:17)**

What Peter saw was a picture from heaven showing him all kinds of four footed animals, as well as reptiles of the earth and birds of the air. God used visual imagery to communicate with him so that he would be able to understand the meaning.

Visual imagery is a powerful method of communication. The picture often stays in our mind for an extended length of time, or even longer, sometimes lasting for a whole lifetime.

Jesus used many different forms of visual imagery by using parables, to enable people to understand the profound meaning behind his teachings. For example, in **Matthew 6:26, 28** he encouraged the people to look at the birds of the air and the lilies of the field. *"Jesus spoke all these things to the crowd in parables; He did not say anything to them without using a parable."* **(Matthew 13:34)**

When Jesus was on this earth ministering, He saw visions all the time. He said, *"I tell you the truth, the Son can do nothing by himself, He can do only what He sees His Father doing, because whatever the Father does the Son also does.* **(John 5:19)**

Jesus saw visions all the time, He saw the open heaven and saw what the Father was doing and He did accordingly.

*Paul and his companions travelled throughout the region of Phrygia and Galatia, having been kept by the Holy Spirit from preaching the word in the province of Asia. When they came to the border of Mysia, they tried to enter Bithynia, but the Spirit of Jesus would not allow them to. So they passed by Mysia and went down to Troas. During the night Paul had a vision of a man of Macedonia standing and begging him "come over to Macedonia and help us." After Paul had seen the vision, we got ready at once to leave for Macedonia, concluding that God had called us to preach the gospel to them.* **(Acts 16:6-10)**

When Paul left Antioch for his second missionary journey, he did not receive any special direction from the Lord but acted upon what he thought was right. He made multiple mistakes. Paul's first attempt to move to Asia was blocked by the Holy Spirit. Although the Holy Spirit did not speak to him in a loud voice or specifically instruct Paul on where to go, the Holy Spirit prevented him from preaching there. When Paul moved again, this time to Bithynia, he got it wrong again. However, the Holy Spirit still did not give him precise instructions as to where exactly he should go. Paul moved to Troas, and only then did God finally give him a vision of Macedonia. When Paul received the vision, he understood the meaning immediately and travelled to the place.

God used visions to communicate with Paul. When Paul saw the vision of the Macedonian man, he was able to recognise that this was where God was calling him to go.

Another vision I had many years ago was with a group of people at a prayer meeting. During the meeting I noticed one brother was waving his hand and praying passionately. Although there were no issues with this man, God told me that this man would not remain in this church for long and that he would leave. I later shared my vision with some of my leaders and after some time, the brother left the Church.

On one occasion when I was driving to a meeting in Wembley, I was not sure where I was going and ended up driving round and round Wembley Stadium. Suddenly, I had a vision of myself standing in a football stadium. I had the strong feeling that one day; I would stand in a football stadium like this. At the time, this vision seemed impossible, but I treasured it in my heart. A few years later, in the year of 2007, I received an invitation from a major prayer ministry in London called the Global Day of Prayer. This event attracts thousands of churches across the UK for united prayer for the nation, I was asked to say a prayer in Cantonese on the stage of West Ham football stadium. Holding a microphone, I stood on the stage in the stadium and prayed!

When I was a new Christian, a young boy from the Church I was attending came to my shop riding his bicycle. He told me that during the Sunday worship service, he saw me in a vision standing on the church platform with Jesus. After hearing this, I was scared because I thought only those who had died could see Jesus. I thought to myself, how can this be so?

You may ask, what is vision? To put it simply, a vision is a picture that God puts in your mind that you see in your spirit. This happens to me very often, especially when in prayer and meditation, where suddenly God drops a picture, or a place or an images in my mind and I can see it with the eyes of my heart.

Ask God to give you a vision that you can see with your spiritual eyes.

Do not be surprised by visions. When we receive them, we may not be able to fully understand the meaning of it at the time, but God will help us step by step. The vision we receive may not come true at once, it may happen after many years. In the Bible, God gave Abraham a vision, saying *"Look up at the sky and count the stars, if indeed you can count them." Then he said to him "so shall your offspring be"* **(Genesis 15:5)**

*I will surely bless you and make your descendants as numerous as the stars in the sky and as the sand on the seashore. Your descendants will take possession of the cities of their enemies.* **(Genesis 22:17)**

This vision God gave to Abraham came to fulfilment after many years.

The vision God has given you could be fulfilled immediately, in the near future or many years after. Remember, when God gives you a vision, He will fulfil it according to His perfect timing.

We need to write down the vision that God gives us and pray about it.

*God asked John to write down what he has seen. "Write on a scroll what you see and send it to the seven churches."* **(Revelation 1:11)**

*"Write, therefore, what you have seen, what is now and what will take place later."* **(Revelation 1:19)**

# Chapter 8
# God speaks to us through dreams

*But God came to Abimelech in a dream one night and said to him. "You are as good as dead because of the woman you have taken; she is a married woman."* **(Genesis 20:3)**

God used dreams to warn Abimelech not to touch Sarah. Abimelech recognised God's voice and responded, even though he was not under the covenant made by God to His people. However, God still spoke to Abimelech through his dreams.

*Jacob left Beersheba and set out for Haran, when he reached a certain place, he stopped for the night because the sun had set. Taking one of the stones there, he put it under his head and lay down to sleep. He had a dream in which he saw a stairway resting on the earth, with its top reaching to heaven, and the angels of God were ascending and descending on it. There above it stood the LORD, and he said: I am the LORD, the God of your father Abraham and the God of Isaac. I will give you and your descendants the land on which you are lying.* **(Genesis 28:10-13)**

Jacob was running away from Esau because Esau was threatening to kill him for stealing his blessings. He was tired after travelling a long journey and did not know what the future would hold. He was desperate, and it was in his desperation that God gave him a dream and spoke to him. He gave him the promise of his

Grandfather Abraham's blessing. God promised Jacob that what He had promised to Abraham would now be transferred to Jacob. He affirmed the promise of protection upon his life. It was God who took the initiative to speak to Jacob through dreams. God knew his need and did not wish for Jacob to remain in fear; therefore he used dreams to speak to him.

*Joseph had a dream, and when he told it to his brothers, they hated him all the more.* (**Genesis 37:5**)

Indeed, God speaks to us through dreams. Joseph had two dreams when he was 17 years old. The dreams revealed to him a future where he would reign over his family, where even his parents would bow before him. The dream was so vivid; it gave him strength even in the face of difficulty. When Joseph had been sold to Egypt, falsely accused and imprisoned for a crime he did not commit, the dream in his heart gave him the strength and purpose to carry on and stand firm. God eventually fulfilled all these dreams in Joseph's life.

God used dreams to speak to Mary's husband Joseph, in Matthew's Gospel chapter one and two, it recorded four dreams that Joseph had received, God used these dreams to protect and guide him.

One of the most exciting dreams I have had was when I first became a Christian. On a Sunday at around five to six o' clock in the morning, I had a dream which revealed to me every detail of the upcoming Sunday service. In my dream, the pastor was preaching on the Ten Commandments, when he took off his jacket and threw it to the senior pastor. As the worship team were returning to the stage after he had finished preaching, he also waved his hand to signal them to come down from the stage. When I woke up, I went to church as usual. I shared with my wife and friends the dream that I had had. On that day, everything that had happened during my dream happened in exactly the same way at Sunday service. I was overwhelmed with joy.

Some may wonder why God uses dreams to communicate with us. My belief is that He does this out of his love, to train us to recognise His voice even as we sleep.

God does not want us to stay where we are. He uses different methods to communicate with us in order to train us and help us grow. A few weeks after I received the first dream, I had another one that also came true. In that dream, I saw the pastor preaching the word of God but the atmosphere of the church was making it very difficult for him to preach effectively. Therefore, he decided to end his sermon half way through the message. Again, this dream became reality the very next Sunday. Before service started, I again relayed the details of my dream to my wife and friends, and again, the service turned out exactly as it had been in my dream.

Often, God resorts to speaking to us through dreams because we are too busy to hear him properly. He wants to speak to us and draw our attention to certain matters, but we are too preoccupied with our own agendas. One of the best moments to speak to us is when we are able to be still and quiet. This is usually when we are sleeping, we are less likely to be distracted by other things and this is a time that God would use to speak to us.

*For God does speak- now one way, now another- though man may not perceive it. In a dream, in a vision of the night, when deep sleep falls on men as they slumber in their beds, He may speak in their ears and terrify them with warnings, to turn from wrongdoing and keep him from pride, to preserve his soul from the pit, his life from perishing by the sword.* **(Job 33:14-18)**

It is worth highlighting that not every dream is from God. Some stem from our own personal worries and thoughts, as our minds continue to ponder on all matters even as we sleep. I am sure you understand what I am talking about. If the dream is from God, you will usually remember it, or the dream will come back to your mind again.

We can ask God to give us dreams before we go to sleep, it is He who grants us sleep and wakes us up every morning, we don't have dream from God because we do not ask, if we ask God to give us dream, we will receive it. In the book of Joel and Acts it states:

"In the last days, God says, I will pour out my Spirit on all people. Your sons and daughters will prophesy, your young men will see visions, your old men will dream dreams." **(Acts 2:17)**

## *Do not ignore dreams, write it down and pray about it. Also ask God to speak to us through dreams*

# Chapter 9

# God speaks to us through His creation

*The heavens declare the glory of God; the skies proclaim the work of his hands. Day after day they pour forth speech; night after night they display knowledge. There is no speech or language where their voice is not heard. Their voice goes out into all the earth, their words to the ends of the world. In the heavens he has pitched a tent for the sun. Which is like a bridegroom coming forth from his pavilion, like a champion rejoicing to run his course. It rises at one end of the heavens and makes its circuit to the other; nothing is hidden from its heat.* **(Psalm 19:1-6)**

*The earth is the Lord's, and everything in it, the world, and all who live in it.* **(Psalm 24:1)**

Everything belongs to the Lord; he can use anything to communicate with us.

The sea resounds, the rivers clap their hands, the mountains sing for joy. God can use a donkey to speak in a human voice and the sky displays His **GLORY**.

*The voice of the Lord is over the waters;
the God of glory thunders,
the Lord thunders over the mighty waters.
The voice of the Lord is powerful;
the voice of the Lord is majestic.
The voice of the Lord breaks the cedars;
the Lord breaks in pieces the cedars of Lebanon.
He makes Lebanon skip like a calf,
Sirion like a young wild ox.*

*The voice of the Lord strikes
with flashes of lightning.
The voice of the Lord shakes the desert;
the Lord shakes the Desert of Kadesh.
The voice of the Lord twists the oaks
and strips the forests bare.
And in his temple all cry, "Glory!"* **(Psalm 29:3-9)**

*For since the creation of the world God's invisible qualities, his eternal power and divine nature, have been clearly seen, so that men are without excuse.* **(Romans 1:20)**

I had a lot of questions to ask God when I first became a Christian. A few weeks after accepted Jesus, I knew in my heart that I trusted God, but I realised that I still had many unanswered questions on my mind. I wondered why wars were happening, why poverty and starvation were still prevalent. I questioned why so many bad things were happening in this world, and this made me feel sad and downcast. I simply had no answers to all these questions in my head. One afternoon, I was walking in the shopping centre with my wife when I noticed a shoe shop called Faith. Although I had been to that place many times before, I had never seen this store. As I walked past, God opened my eyes on that day to see the name clearly: **Faith.** My heart was pounding and I knew that this was the voice of God. He was telling me to have faith in Him.

Our previous church office was located in the red light district in Soho. On one occasion, as I was leaving the office, I stopped outside one of the shops. It was completely empty except for a few pieces of artwork. However, they were artistic paintings, not sexual imagery! As I stared at the beautiful paintings, a man came outside and invited me in. I did not dare to enter as the shop was located in the red light district of Soho. My mind cried out at me not to enter, but a voice inside me told me to go in. I was not sure what would happen to me if I went into the shop, but I chose to listen to the voice of the Spirit. I went in and surprisingly the man in the shop introduced himself as an artistic pastor and we had a very good conversation. Later we became friends in the Lord!

A few years ago at our church Easter conference, one person decided to accept Jesus. The moment after he finished saying the prayer of salvation, heavy snow began to fall. This was in April. It is extremely unusual for it to snow in Greater London in April, as we are usually well into spring. However, aside from this extraordinary phenomenon, what was even more amazing was that the snow only fell in our particular area for a few minutes. I am certain that God spoke to us. He used the snow to tell us our sins have been wiped away and now we are whiter than snow. We are clean!

In the week of my baptism, two pigeons flew into my shop, I didn't understand the meaning of the pigeons at that time, because I was a new Christian at only four months old. I now understand it was God speaking through the pigeons, meaning the Holy Spirit is with me.

Many years ago, during one of our church teaching courses, we were training our church members on how to listen to God's voice. When we began to practice hearing His voice, over 40 pigeons suddenly flew over to the windows of our building. This was exceptionally strange, we did not know where all these pigeons had suddenly come from.

God speaks through His creation. Sometimes when we look at the sky, the beautiful flower in the garden or the rainbow in the sky can fill our hearts with awe.

The heavens declare His glory. When men sinned against God, they had become very wicked. The bible said in **(Genesis 6: 5, 7)** *The LORD saw how great man's wickedness on the earth had become, and that every inclination of the thoughts of his heart was only evil all the time. So God said: "I will wipe mankind whom I have created, from the face of the earth."* God used the flood to punish that generation but saved the family of Noah. However, after the flood, God placed a rainbow in the sky to remind us of His covenant. God continues to speak to us using rainbows to this very day. He uses it to serve as a reminder of His love, mercy and faithfulness.

And God said, *"This is the sign of the covenant I am making between me and you and everything living creature with you, a covenant for all generation to come: I have set my rainbow in the clouds, and it will be the sign of the covenant between me and the Earth. Whenever I bring clouds over the earth and the rainbow appears in the clouds, I will remember my covenant between me and you and all living creatures of every kind. Never again will the water become a flood to destroy all life. Whenever the rainbow appears in the clouds, I will see it and remember the everlasting covenant between God and all living creatures of every kind on the earth.* **(Genesis 9:12-16)**

# *God speaks to us through His creation; He can use everything in this world to communicate with us*

# Chapter 10

# God speaks to us through our five senses

God speaks through the five senses that He created us with. These are what we **SEE, SMELL, HEAR, TOUCH** and **TASTE**.

*For you created my inmost being; you knit me together in my mother's womb. I praise you because I am fearfully and wonderfully made; your works are wonderful, I know that full well. My frame was not hidden from you when I was made in the secret place, when I was woven together in the depths of the earth. Your eyes saw my unformed body; all the days ordained for me were written in your book before one of them came to be.* **(Psalm 139:13-16)**

# SEE:

*Ears that hear and eyes that see, the Lord has made them both.* **(Proverbs 20:12)**

*Does he who implanted the ear not hear? Does he who formed the eye not see?* **(Psalm 94:9)**

*When King of Aram sent an army to surround the city to get Elisha, his servant got up in the morning and saw this, he asked what shall we do? Then Elisha prayed, "O LORD, open his eyes so he may see." Then the LORD opened the servant's eyes, and he looked and saw the hills full of horse and chariots of fire all around Elisha.* **(2 Kings 6:17)**

God opened Elisha's servant's eyes, so that he can see things that were hidden. God often opens our eyes, so that we may see something that we were unable to see before or maybe saw but did not pay attention to. Sometimes, God may suddenly open our eyes to a situation and we notice something entirely different. This is called **revelation**! This is when something has now, not just been **recognised** but has now been **revealed**.

*I pray that the eyes of your heart may be enlightened in order that you may know the hope to which he has called you, the riches of his glorious inheritance in his holy people.* **(Ephesians 1:18)**

Moses saw an unusual thing in **(Exodus 3:2)** the burning bush, the fire from within a bush. Moses saw that though the bush was on fire it did not burn up. God used this unusual experience to draw Moses' attention.

*The Word of the LORD came to me:" what do you see, Jeremiah?" "I see the branch of an almond tree," I replied.* **(Jeremiah 1:11)**

God asked Jeremiah to **SEE**, what Jeremiah saw has a spiritual meaning, God asked him to see, and Jeremiah saw an almond tree, it was the almond tree that had a Spiritual meaning that God wanted to reveal to him.

God gives us eyes, so that we can see things, and HE does use our five senses to communicate to us.

I remember on one occasion, when I was praying for a man, God highlighted the colour of the clothes of that person to me. The colour of his shirt was a dark colour, which was symbolic at the time for fear; *MY SPIRITUAL EYES* had seen that this person had fear in his life. So I prayed for him and then I asked him if he had fear in his life, he admitted this to be true by nodding his head, and shared that this was precisely why he had come to church for prayer.

# SMELL:

*But thanks be to God, who always leads us in triumphal procession in Christ and through us spreads everywhere the fragrance of the knowledge of him.* (**2 Corinthians 2:14**)

Just one week before our church, Emmanuel Chinese Church newly started; we noticed a new and wonderful fragrance in our home. The smell was so strong that it was spread to every room. Not until a few days later did we find out that the smell was actually from a tree which had never blossomed or grown flowers before. Indeed, we had kept this tree for many years, but only the week before our church started, did flowers blossom from it that emitted such a beautiful fragrance. I believe this was God showing us that we have the special fragrance of His presence. He was telling us that we will spread the aroma of our Lord Jesus Christ everywhere we go. The fragrance from these flowers was so amazing and pleasing to our senses. It really did smell good! The same with God our fragrance must continue to be pleasing to God's senses!

Since that time, I have smelt His aroma on many occasions. Sometimes when I was alone studying His Word and sometimes when I was praying for people, whenever I smell His fragrance I know His presence is there, He wants to draw me closer to Him. It is so wonderful to be in the presence of the Lord that I never want to leave, but wish to continue to enjoy His presence.

God can use our sense of smell to speak to us.

# HEAR:

*He who has an ear, let him hear what the Spirit says to the church.* **(Revelation 3:22)**

God gives us ears, so that we can physically hear voice. We can hear God's voice audibly, though this is usually rare.

*My dear brothers and sisters, take note of this: Everyone should be quick to listen, slow to speak and slow to become angry.* **(James 1:19)**

God also gives us ears to hear spiritually, what I mean is we can hear something supernaturally, in second Kings, God makes some noise so that the enemy can hear it and tremble.

*For the Lord had cause the Arameans to hear the sound of chariots and horses and a great army, so they said to one another, "Look, the king of Israel has hired the Hittite and Egyptian kings to attack us!" so they got up and fled in the dusk and abandoned their tents and their horses and donkeys. They left the camp as it was and ran for their lives.* **(2 Kings 7:6-8)**

In the earlier days of our church, we had a regular meeting hosted at my home where we would practice recognising the presence of God. On one occasion, I asked all who attended to be still and listen to God's voice. Not long after saying this, I started to hear the sound of raindrops falling. Furthermore, everyone else in that room shared that they too could hear the sound of raindrops. This again was the voice of God speaking to us through raindrops falling.

    I enjoy spending time with God, especially during the evening when it is completely quiet and still. There is no one to disturb me, and sometimes I can hear a worship song ringing in my ears. Although no one was playing music or singing, I hear clearly the sound of a worship song, and I am convinced that it is God speaking to me through song.

# TOUCH:

*Suddenly an angel of the Lord appeared and a light shone in the cell, He struck Peter on the side and woke him up, "Quick, get up"! He said, and the chains fell off Peter's wrists.* **(Acts 12:7)**

The angel touched Peter to rescue him from prison. I have also experienced a sensation of physically being touched by God on some occasions. I find this happens more often during ministry time whilst I am praying for others. At these times, I sometimes feel a vibration in my hands, or a sensation of someone touching my shoulder. However, when I turn around to see who it is, there is no one there. This is a supernatural encounter, where God touches my physical being. God uses His touch to communicate with me.

Sometimes when you touch people, God can speak through the touching, He may give you some insight about that person, God wants to speak to us and give us revelation about a particular or personal situation.

# Taste:

*Taste and see that the Lord is good, blessed is the one who takes refuge in him.* **(Psalm 34:8)**

*And He said to me, "Son of man, eat what is before you, eat this scroll I am giving you and fill your stomach with it." So I ate it, and it tasted as sweet as honey in my mouth.* **(Ezekiel 3:1)**

The first time I encountered the spiritual sense of taste was whilst I was ministering to people, I felt a sudden sweet taste in my mouth. This was not because I had been eating something sweet, but it was a supernatural taste of sweetness on my tongue and I knew in my spirit that God was speaking to me through the taste.

It is essential that we exercise our five senses. As a Chinese person most of us are taught to use our five senses from an early age. For example, in Chinese folklore, we often say: *'if our eyelids twitch, someone is thinking or talking about us'*. When our heart is pounding, we are taught to wonder if someone is worrying about us, or if danger is coming. When we go to certain places and our hearts don't feel comfortable, we are taught to recognise this negative atmosphere.

Some may call this superstition, and indeed for non believers it may well be. However, for those who believe in Jesus, we are God's workmanship designed especially to fellowship with Him using all our senses. Do not ignore your five senses, for you have been born into this world with them. God's plan is for you to use your five senses to glorify God. Therefore, He has created us with five senses for a purpose – for us to acknowledge these feelings and use them to speak with Him.

# Chapter 11

# Jesus our example

Jesus started everyday with the Father. He would go up to the mountain every morning to communicate with the Father and hear His voice. He loves the father and the Father loves Him. As a result of this constant communication, they had an intensely deep and intimate relationship.

*Very early in the morning, while it was still dark, Jesus got up, left the house and went off to a solitary place, where he prayed.* **(Mark 1:35)**

In this instance, Jesus prayed throughout the night before He called the twelve disciples. He wanted to know from the Father whom exactly He should call. At that time, there was a large crowd, wishing to follow him, each with their own agenda and motives. Some wished to see miracles; others to listen to His teachings, some merely desired to follow as spectators and had no idea what they truly wanted from following Jesus. To choose the twelve disciples, Jesus needed to hear from the Father.

*One of these days Jesus went out to a mountainside to pray, and spent the night praying to God, when the morning came, he called his disciples to him and chose twelve of them, whom he also designated apostles.* **(Luke 6:12)**

*Jesus said to them, my Father is always at his work to this day, and I too am working.* **(John 5:17)**

Jesus was constantly in fellowship with the Father. As the Father was always at work, Jesus was frequently ministering. Therefore, He needed to be always in direct communication with the Father to know His will in every situation.

*Jesus gave them this answer, "I tell you the truth, the Son can do nothing by himself," he can do only what he sees his Father doing, because whatever the Father does the Son also does. For the Father love the Son and show him all he does. Yes, to your amazement he will show him even greater things than these.* **(John 5:19-20)**

*So Jesus said, "When you have lifted up the Son of Man, then you will know that I am the one I claim to be and that I do nothing on my own but speak just what the Father has taught me.* **(John 8:28)**

Jesus was always hearing from God and made it his practice to hear from God before doing anything else. Even when He was busy ministering to a crowd of people who were following him wherever He went, Jesus found the time to consult the Father alone. He created space in his life to hear from Him. Fellowship with the Father was the top priority in His life.

Hearing from God is important to us all. Jesus heard what the Father was saying and then responded to His Words. His ministry flowed from what He had heard from the Father. Jesus is the best example for us to follow. To spend time alone with God is a choice. It is not always about managing our own agendas, but everything to do with how we set our priorities. If we perceive time alone with God to be important, we will place in a position of importance and priority. We can choose to spend time with Him no matter how busy we are. It is our choice to have fellowship with God and to enjoy His presence. We choose to spend time with Him.

We must cultivate an attitude of hunger and thirst for God in order to be willing to spend time with Him every morning. I encourage you to set aside a regular time to listen to His voice. This may not be easy at the beginning but as you do this more often, you will eventually nurture a habit of spending time with Him and enjoy His presence. Consequently, your life will be transformed and blessed.

# Chapter 12

# How do we know it is God's voice?

There are many voices in the world. These can range from our own voices, to God and the devil. A question that is commonly asked is how can we learn to discern between these voices?

Some of these voices are relatively easy to discern whilst others are harder. If the voice you have heard says something that contradicts the Word of God and is overtly against the will of God, then it does not come from God. For instance if a voice instructs you to steal money because you do not have enough money to pay your mortgage, then you will know instinctively that this is not from God, for it clearly says in the Bible *'You shall not steal.'* **(Exodus 20:15; Ephesians 4:27)**

However, sometimes it is harder to discern. When Jesus was about to go to the cross, he explained to His disciples about His death. Peter rebuked Jesus, stating *"Never, Lord... this shall never happen to you!"* **(Matthew 16:22)**

Peter did not want Jesus to go to the cross to suffer and die. It is easy to understand Peter's heart. He had spent three years with Jesus and had built a close relationship with Him. He did not want Jesus to suffer. However, Jesus knew that the voice was not from the Father nor from Peter. It was from Satan. Jesus rebuked Satan immediately. *'Jesus turned and said to Peter, get behind me Satan, you stumbling block to me, and you do not have in mind the things of God, but the things of men.'* **(Matthew 16:23)**

## GOD'S VOICE NEVER CONTRADICTS HIS WRITTEN WORD

If the voice that you heard tells you something which contradicts the written Word of God, it is definitely not from God. God's voice will never tell us to do something that is contrary to that, written in the Holy Scripture. God's truth is always consistent.

Jesus said: *I tell you the truth, until heaven and earth disappear, not the smallest letter, not the least stroke of a pen, will by any means disappear from the law until everything is accomplished.* **(Matthew 5:18)**

I met a woman who came to me and explained that she believed that it was the will of God for her to marry a non-believer, although she said she heard the voice of God telling her to marry a non-believer. We know that God would never tell her to marry a non-believer.

Many years ago, a person shared with me his personal experience of hearing God's voice. He wanted to move out of his current accommodation to a different area. He heard God telling him to buy a big and expensive house. When I enquired whether he could afford the mortgage, he replied that God would provide. After just a few months, he moved out of this property and bought an ex-council house. His explanation was that God wanted him to preach the good news to the poor. After yet another few months, he moved to the seaside. This time he said that God wished him to move to the seaside as there were many good schools there for his son. All we can say is that there was very little spiritual insight into all these movements. Whatever this person chose to do, he would use God's name to assert his decision as the correct one. This shows us that this individual like many may have had some problems in the way he was hearing God's voice. It is likely that he was not able to discern between God's 'voice' and his 'own'. Therefore, it is important that in all circumstances, we are able to clearly discern God's voice from others.

## GOD'S VOICE WILL NEVER LEAD US AWAY FROM HIM OR HIS WORD.

If the voice that we have heard tells us not to worship God, or draws us away from His church, no matter how accurate the content is, we need to know this: God will not tell us to do something that results in us to be separated from Him. I have had people share with me that God has instructed them to work seven days a week to earn more money and therefore they have no time to go to church to worship God. These thoughts are certainly not from God as they are drawing His people away from Him. This is evident in **(Deuteronomy 13:1-3)** where it states *if a prophet or one who foretells by dreams, appears among you and announces to you a miraculous sign or wonder, and if the sign or wonder of which he has spoken takes place, and he says, "let us follow other gods" (gods you have not known and let us worship them," you must not listen to the words of that prophet or dreamer. The Lord your God is testing you to find out whether you love him with all your heart and with all your soul.*

## GOD'S VOICE BRINGS JOY, PEACE, LOVE AND ENCOURAGEMENT; HIS VOICE DRAWS US CLOSER TO HIMSELF

God's voice brings peace and joy. *Rejoice in the Lord always, I will say it again: Rejoice! Let your gentleness be evident to all. The Lord is near. Do not be anxious about anything, but in everything, by prayer and petition with thanksgiving, present your requests to God, and the peace of God, which transcends all understanding, will*

*Guard your hearts and your minds in Christ Jesus.* **(Philippians 4:4-7)**

Our God is not a God of confusion. He will not make us worry and confuse us with His Word.

*For God is not a God of disorder but of peace.*
**(1 Corinthians 14:33)**

When His voice comes to us, we have peace in our hearts, for we know in our hearts that it is from God. The more we hear His voice, the easier it becomes to recognise it. Our spirit will recognise His voice when He speaks, as if we are answering a phone call from a close friend, we can recognise their voice immediately. So it is with God, the more time we spend with Him, the more accustomed we shall become to hearing His voice.

## RESPOND BY FAITH

To know the voice of God requires faith. What is faith? In **Hebrews 11:1** it states that faith is believing the unseen, it is being sure of what we hope for and certain of what we do not see.

*It is by grace you have been saved, through faith, and this is not from yourselves, it is the gift of God.*
**(Ephesians 2:8)**

How can we be sure that we are saved? It is by faith, as it is stated above in the scripture. We are saved because of what Jesus has done on the cross. We have not seen it with our eyes but by faith we believe that He paid for our sins. The same applies to hearing God's voice.

We live by faith, not by sight. **(2 Corinthians 5:7)**

## WE NEED FAITH TO RECEIVE WHAT WE HEAR.

*Faith comes from hearing the message, and the message is heard through the word of Christ.* **(Romans 10:17)**

Responding to God requires faith. If we do not receive the Word by faith, the thief will come to steal, kill and destroy what has been given to us. Jesus stated that His sheep can hear his voice, and He came so that we (His sheep) may have abundant life. It is important to know that the thief (satan) attempts to steal the promises given to us when we doubt God's voice! Therefore do not doubt when you think you hear God's voice. Respond to His voice with faith, and it will be yours. Our first reaction to God's voice is often to wonder if this is our own imagination speaking to us. Although most people will naturally think in this way, we must understand that faith is required to respond to His Word. There are many things that we do not yet fully understand and that is why we need faith to respond to God.

Paul's words in Corinthians and Hebrews explain this clearly.

*We see but a poor reflection as in a mirror, then I shall know fully, even as I am fully known.* **(1 Corinthians 13:12)**

*Faith is being sure of what we hope for and certain of what we do not see.* **(Hebrews 11:1)**

*Jesus said: "The thief comes only to steal and kill and destroy, I have come that they may have life, and have it to the full.* **(John 10:10)**

Like I stated earlier it is important that we know the thief (satan) will come and steal the Word away if we have doubt in God's voice. So do not doubt when we hear His voice. Respond to it by faith and it will be yours.

# Chapter 13

# Practical ways of hearing His voice

*It is not difficult to hear from God but we sometimes complicate matters by attaching too many rules for ourselves. We ought to be confident and not doubt when hearing His voice.*

## BE CONFIDENT

*But when he asks, he must believe and not doubt, because he who doubts is like a wave of the sea, blown and tossed by the wind. That man should not think he will receive anything from the Lord, he is a double-minded man, unstable in all he does.* (**James 1:6-8**)

A double-minded person is dangerous. Such a person is not stable. He cannot make up his mind, but is constantly changing his mind. The characteristics of such an individual include one who will make a decision to go left, then decide to turn right, then left again, bouncing between left and right like a yoyo. A double minded person is not confident of which way he should turn. Therefore we must be certain, knowing that our confidence is not in ourselves, but in the Lord.

He has opened a new and living way to us, so that we can come to His presence. No one can come to the Father except through him.

*Yet to all who did receive him, to those who*

*believed in his name, he gave the right to become children of God* **(John 1:12)**

*Now, we are children of God.* **(1 John 3:1)**

As a child of God, we can hear His voice based on a father and son/daughter relationship. We should focus on building a relationship and not on our own negative thoughts. People may say to you, *"you can never hear God's voice because you have not confessed your sins. You must confess all your sins before hearing."* Whilst there is some truth in this saying, it is not completely correct. If we have some known sins and have deliberately sinned against God, then we must confess our sins and repent.

However, we should not focus only on our sins, or we will spend our entire lives repeatedly confessing our sins. The devil will remind you non-stop of your sins. For example, he might remind you that you have done something wrong last week. You will then confess your sin, and then devil will remind you of an incident two weeks ago when you stepped on someone's foot and did not say sorry. The devil will capture you in a whirlpool of confessions, where you are continually confessing and repenting. In the meantime he will keep reminding you of your hidden sins, to find any areas of offense. The devil will never stop attacking you, he will keep beating you over the head with your sins and guilt until you are unable to stand it anymore. You might find yourself so absorbed in his attempts to poison your heart, only to realise that you have completely wasted a huge amount of time and are still not any closer to hearing God's voice! Do not focus only on your sins.

However, some may ask – what if you do forget to confess one small sin? Does this mean you will never be able to hear our Heavenly Father's voice?

Remember, all of our sins have already been forgiven. The devil wishes us to focus on our own sins so that he can make us feel unworthy to approach God. He wants to make us feel guilty and uses every tactic to prevent us from coming before God. The devil is a liar. The truth is Jesus died for our sins on the cross. Jesus paid for all our sins: past, present and future. Jesus used His life to pay for our sins so that we could come boldly into His presence.

*The sin which condemn us has been paid by Jesus on the Calvary, we now have confidence to come to God. As in* **(1 John 3:21)** *state: Dear friends, if our heart do not condemn us, we have confidence before God.*

*Forgive each other just as in Christ God forgave you* **(Ephesians 4:32)**

We should not concentrate on sin because we are now clean, righteous and holy. We have become saints. Our identity is now a child of God. We belong to Him, and we can come into His presence to listen to His voice and fellowship with our Heavenly Father.

We must be confident that we can definitely hear His voice. When we focus on our relationship with our Heavenly Father instead of our sin (which Jesus has already paid the price for on the cross) God opens a new and living way for us to come to Him so that we may hear His voice.

## BE STILL

Like I said before it's important to set aside a portion of your time either in the early morning, evening or anytime during the day to listen to God's voice. It does not matter when, as long as you set apart a portion of your time daily to fellowship with God. The duration of the time does not matter as different individuals prefer to spend a different length of time with God. The most important thing is that we create a platform for us to communicate with God and listen to His voice.

A quiet place is preferable as it is generally easier to feel peace in your heart. Peaceful environments can make it easier to tune into God.

Noisy places like markets or crowded areas may prove distracting and prevent you from hearing His voice. In addition, it is best to find a place where you can concentrate without any distractions or disturbances. In the world we live in, many of us are very busy with life in general, but remember there is always a time to just close the door, switch off your mobile phone and be still in the presence of God.

The Bible encourages us to be still. This is evident when it says *be still and know that he is Lord.* **(Psalm 46:10)**

When we are still, our mind can focus on Jesus completely. This helps us to fix our eyes on Him alone. The Bible says *'Let us fix our eyes on Jesus, the author and perfecter of our faith.'* **(Hebrew 12:1-2)**

Once you have done this, then begin to read and meditate on His word. You will be surprised to hear His voice, once you spend a portion of your time daily with God. Your life will never be the same again.

## BE NATURAL

Do not force yourself to hear God's voice. Some people try to force God to speak to them through prayer and fasting. This is not the right attitude. If we force ourselves, we will only feel pressure and guilt if we do not hear from God.

Furthermore, do not try to force God to speak to you by the limits of your own imagination or by your preferred methods. Simply put, do not limit how God can speak to you. God can speak to you through many different channels and methods, and it is up to Him to choose which method He desires at any given time. His ways are higher than ours.

Be natural, be yourself. There is no pressure. If God has not spoken to you today, that is totally fine. Do not force yourself into the mindset that you must hear from God every second. If you are unable to hear His voice today, try again tomorrow or even the day after. Never stop trying because God's voice will definitely come at some point. You are his beloved child. He may speak to you whilst you are cooking, washing the dishes or waiting for a bus. Remember God can speak to you at any time or place.

## DO NOT SET LIMITATIONS FOR GOD JUST BE NATURAL

Finally, God is God. There are absolutely no precise formulas or methods that automatically ensure that you will hear His voice. Do not be limited by sitting postures, locations or times that can facilitate this. Hearing God's voice is not about following a formula, but about developing a relationship. This means learning to walk, fellowship and communicate with Him.

God's voice is not limited. He can speak to us in a variety of ways. Our Creator knows us the best. He alone knows the best way to communicate with us so that we may hear His voice. God speaks differently to each person. Each individual's experience of hearing God's voice will be entirely unique. God has created you to be unique and special, no one else in this world is exactly the same as you. As you are unique and awesome in His eyes, He will speak to you in a unique and awesome way, especially designed for you. Although God spoke to Moses in a burning bush (**Exodus 3:2**) God is unlikely to speak to you in the same way. Paul heard a voice and saw a flashing light around him on the way to Damascus (**Acts 9:3-7**), however God may choose not to speak to us using these methods either.

The experience of others is to allow us to understand that God has a variety of methods by which He can communicate with us. Another individual's encounter with God serves only to enrich our understanding of His voice. Only God is all knowing and therefore He alone, knows the best way to communicate with us. Some of us are introverts, whilst others are extroverts, some of us are more talkative, whilst others are more reserved.

There are people who can hear God's voice better through the reading of His Word. Others may find it easier when they look up at the sky. Some can tune in with God and hear His voice better when they are in quiet places. Some people enjoy staying quiet, as this allows creative ideas to flow into their mind. Some may see visions, draw pictures, dance or mediate. Their minds can tune in with God in quietness.

However others may find it difficult to stay still even for one minute. Though their body is still, their mind is still travelling to the four corners of the earth, or even considering their next delicious meal. These kinds of people will find it challenging to hear God in stillness. However God can use other ways to speaks to them.

I hope this helps you to understand that only God knows which way is best suited for us to hear His voice.

# Chapter 14
# Hearing God's Voice

*(My personal encounter with God)*

God has always been training me to hear His voice even to this very day, I am still learning to hear His voice.

He loves us and desire us to grow in our spiritual lives continually so that we may know Him better and deepen our relationship with Him, God always wants to speak to us!

My personal encounter with God is that whenever He teaches me something, I respond immediately. Consequently He is able to keep teaching me new things from one stage to another. He creates a hunger in my heart so that I would continually desire more of Him. This is what we need, a hunger for God, this hunger and fire inside of us must never die down, we continue to come to His presence and maintain a hunger for God always! Like the Psalmist, he thirsts for God. *As the deer pants for streams of water, so my soul pants for you O God. My soul thirsts for God, for the living God. When can I go and meet with God.* **(Psalm 42:1-2)**

The most dangerous thing in life that could ever happen is that we lose our hunger, passion and fire for God. It is also this reason that I regularly remind myself not to lose this fire in my life.

In the contrary, the most exciting thing in life is hearing God's voice and knowing His presence.

One of my recent encounter with God happened when the church was celebrating my birthday in 2015. The celebration took place on Sunday at a hotel, and just on Monday after, I received a very strange email on my church email account, which says:

*"Dear Pastor Bobby*
*Wondering if you are the Bobby I knew from Crofton Park? If so, I would love to re-new contact."*

*I emailed him back. And responded "Yes, I am the Bobby you know.*

I knew this person when I first became a Christian. He left the church I had been attending after a few months to study in Bible College and later became a missionary in USA.

I had not seen him or contacted him after he left for USA. Now, 29 years later, he suddenly wanted to look for me. I found this very strange.

In my reply to him, I asked: *"how did you find me? And why are you looking for me?*

He responded and said:
*"The Lord brought you into my mind quite specifically yesterday so we searched for you online."*

It was on Sunday that God told him to look for me. God laid a burden about me in his heart, which was the reason he tried to search for me on google. He did not even know why he wanted to find me, except that he obeyed the voice of God. I later told him that Sunday was my birthday, and the church celebrated with me in a hotel.

I believe this was a message from God saying to me that He loves me and is watching over me.

God was speaking to me through this man on my birthday. It was the best birthday present I received from heaven. The voice of God!

## HEARING GOD'S VOICE IS EXCITING

Hearing God's voice is all about relationship, it is our relationship with the King of Kings and the Lord of Lords, the Creator of all things, and He is our Heavenly Father. Jesus continues to invite us to come to His presence and hear his voice. He said *"Here I am! I stand at the door and knock. If anyone hears my voice and opens the door, I will come in and eat with him, and he with me."* **(Revelation 3:20).**

*"Come to me, all you who are weary and burdened, and I will give you rest. Take my yoke upon you and learn from me, for I am gentle and humble in heart, and you will find rest for your souls. For my yoke is easy and my burden is light."* **(Matthew 11:28-30)**

Jesus wants us to hear His voice and fellowship with Him because it is only His voice that can satisfy our thirsty soul. His voice can help us when we are in need and in trouble and it is only His voice that can guide us into the right path of life and it is His voice that can give us joy when we are sad, give us peace when we face difficulty, give us love when we feel lonely.

I pray this book will help you to hear God clearly and excite you to want more of God in your life and build a close intimate relationship with Him.

Open your heart and ears, be ready to listen to His voice, and to respond to Him.

*Then a cloud appeared and enveloped them, and a voice came from the cloud: "This is my Son, whom I love. Listen to him."* **(Mark 9:7)**

We want to come to His presence and listen to Him, just like David, he wanted to seek God:

*One thing I ask of the LORD, this is what I seek: that I may dwell in the house of the LORD all the days of my life, to gaze upon the beauty of the LORD and to seek him in his temple.* **(Psalm 27:4)**

Like Samuel, he just wanted to hear God's voice:

*The LORD came and stood there, calling as at the other times, "Samuel! Samuel!" Then Samuel said, "Speak, for your servant is listening."* **(1 Samuel 3:10)**

Like Mary, she just wanted to listen to Jesus:

She had a sister called Mary, who sat at the Lord's feet listening to what He said. **(Luke 10:39)**

But one thing is needed. Mary has chosen what is better, and it will not be taken away from her. **(Luke 10:42)**

Like Paul, he just wanted Jesus, and nothing else:

*What is more, I consider everything a loss compared to the surpassing greatness of knowing Christ Jesus my Lord, for whose sake I have lost all things. I consider them rubbish, that I may gain Christ.* **(Philippians 3:8)**

# Invitation To Salvation

If you want to become a Christian believer and follow Jesus right now you can pray this prayer below:

*Dear Lord Jesus, I accept you as my Lord and personal saviour. I repent and ask that you please forgive me of all of my sins. Today I make a choice to follow you. Please come into my life and guide me, speak to me, so that I can hear your voice. In Jesus name I pray. Amen.*

But what does it say? "The word is near you; it is in your mouth and in your heart," that is, the message concerning faith that we proclaim: If you declare with your mouth, "Jesus is Lord," and believe in your heart that God raised him from the dead, you will be saved. For it is with your heart that you believe and are justified, and it is with your mouth that you profess your faith and are saved. As Scripture says, "Anyone who believes in him will never be put to shame. For there is no difference between Jew and Gentile—the same Lord is Lord of all and richly blesses all who call on him, for,

"Everyone who calls on the name of the Lord will be saved. "How, then, can they call on the one they have not believed in? And how can they believe in the one of whom they have not heard? And how can they hear without someone preaching to them? And *how can anyone preach unless they are sent? As it is written: "How beautiful are the feet of those who bring good news!" But not all the Israelites accepted the good news. For Isaiah says, "Lord, who has believed our message?" Consequently, faith comes from hearing the message, and the message is heard through the word about Christ.* **(Romans 10:8-17)**

> *"The* Lord *bless you*
> *and keep you;*
> *The* Lord *make his face shine on you*
> *and be gracious to you;*
> *the* Lord *turn his face toward you*
> *and give you peace."* **(Numbers 6:24-26)**

**Rev. Dr. Bobby Sung**
**www.ecclondon.com**

# Hearing God's Voice Notes

# Hearing God's Voice Notes

# Hearing God's Voice Notes

# Hearing God's Voice Notes

# Hearing God's Voice Notes

# Hearing God's Voice Notes

Lightning Source UK Ltd.
Milton Keynes UK
UKOW04f1009080715

254746UK00002B/24/P